the GREECE I love

the

GREECE I love

Photography by ROBERT DESCHARNES

Introduction by JACQUES DE LACRETELLE
de l'Académie Française

Titles by ANDRÉ FRAIGNEAU

Text by MICHEL DÉON

TUDOR PUBLISHING COMPANY

New York

The wonderful thing about one's first visit to Greece is to find it just as one imagined it would be and yet it never ceases to surprise. This contradiction arises from Greece's many faces. It is grave and pensive, inducing a state of awed contemplation before an art which has attained perfection. And it is light, airy, smiling—freed from academic doctrines. Its legend and its past glitter in an abstract world and its body lives in the light of this world. The arrival in Greece has unforgettable impact! One expected to land on an abandoned shore to stroll among marble debris. But in that antique beauty there was once such a burst of life, such a strong pact with nature that present-day images are as captivating as the monuments. The landscape belongs to history but poetry has stolen it. And the metamorphosis takes place before our eyes.

At Delphi, gods lurk in the trunks of olive trees and in the Phedriades ravine. Perhaps they also circle in the sky in the form of eagles.

At Attica, the earth is reddened by the blood of Marathon. Near Salamis, the horizon is quiet and flat. It is the calm which comes after victory.

At Mycenae, the hillock where Agammemnon was slaughtered has forever remained veiled in gray. At Tiryns, that mischievous child Herakles played with his blocks and left them scattered everywhere.

Greece satisfies every desire and every appetite. For idealists there is Olympia and its peaceful truce. For advocates of strong-arm methods there is Sparta. However, such advocates should pause to reflect: of Sparta not a stone remains. And the hoplites lances have become Eurotas reeds.

There is a Greece which haunts the dramatists and a Greece which is the dream of colleges of education. There is also the one which glorifies sports champions. Cradle of democracy (as we are constantly reminded), let us not forget that it is also the couch of Alcibiades. It started us on rhetoric and taught us measure. The fountain of Castalia inspired poets and the Ilissos loosened Plato's tongue. Enthusiasm was born in Greece and overran its boundaries like the foliage of the olive tree. But next to it, reason grew strong like a cypress. All of that is written in its soil, in the lines of its landscapes, on the pediments of its temples.

Greece goes to the head. Its waters have swallowed up many an enthusiast like Byron. Before its erect columns a rationalist declaims lyrically and an atheist poet composes canticles.

* * *

"Antiquity is the bread of professors," wrote Goncourt somewhat spitefully. And it is true that the soil of Greece is littered with famous words. Its columns invite parallels.

In France Chateaubriand kindled the flame. "At Sparta, the fortified soul seems to rise and swell. At Athens, one can conceive of the perfection of man considered as an intelligent being." And here is his high C: "On passing from the ruins of Lacedaemon to the ruins of Athens I felt that I would have liked to die with Leonidas and live with Pericles."

Conflicting desires except in the sonority of the words! For the elegant and harmonious but somewhat cold Lamartine the Parthenon is "the most perfect poem in stone on the face of the earth." Before the Acropolis Renan kneeled and Maurras loved. Although he never set foot in Greece, Goethe set the meeting of Helen and Faust there in the second *Faust*. He described Mistra and its fortified castle (which later enchanted Barrès) with the precision of his compatriot Baedeker: "There you see columns and colonnettes, arches and vaulted arches, balconies, galleries where one may see outside and inside, and coats-of-arms."

These lofty guides should be sufficient. But we are living in a time where books have little place. The image has replaced the phrase and the Rolleiflex film the library. This invitation to a voyage in Greece, transmitted by illustrious authors, is as outdated as a "Dear Reader" would be at the beginning of this book. All that needs be said is, "Traveler, look about you."

* * *

Look first at the light. It resembles nothing you have ever seen until this moment. It covers objects with a transparent veil which subdues the brilliance while heightening the sharpness of outline. It is a changing light which, according to the hour, reveals a different substance.

Nothing too vivid or coarse and yet nothing soft nor blurred. All that it touches becomes eloquent and intelligible. The shore, the shaded line of a hill, the grove of olive trees seem animated, enriched by it.

For those who seek in nature subjects for thought, subtle differences rather than contrasts, for those who love to dream on the edge of reality this light will perform miracles. I believe it has much to do with the extraordinary ingenuity of Greek mythology. It sharpened the visual powers of this inventive and gifted little people. It intoxicated their imagination. From dawn to night, on sea, on the road, it made them live in a sort of constant enchantment.

* * *

Now look at the sea. It belongs to Hellenic poets and prosaists. All of them described and addressed it in extravagant and accurate epithets. Like the ancient chorus it accompanies their tale. It is the soul of all the Greek people. Take the sailor, the one from Nauplia, the one from the Piraeus, the one from the islands, as he climbs the mast, unties the ropes and steps into his boat. It is Ulysses. He is chuckling over his time-old masquerade. For centuries no one has recognized him in the guise of Poseidon.

* * *

Then look to the mountains. They have a palpable appearance.

They are living. They are sleeping Cyclops, reclining nymphs, on whom a fleece of short and vigorous vegetation is growing. None is very high and all will overwhelm you. Olympus has remained less accessible than the Himalayas. The Taygetus looks like a mass of steel. Parnassus can be climbed in summer only and with goatherds who can pick up Pan's trace. At Delos, the Cynthos, Apollo's birthplace, is only 300 feet high. But from its summit one reigns over all the Cyclades.

The hills of Athens are a thing apart. They gave birth to the Acropolis. Like a tribe of nursemaids, they keep constant watch over it. Hence the harmonious forms, the absence of disorder, the unity of lines and purity of color. One of them, however, the Pentelicon mountain, bears a gaping wound in its flank from having offered pieces of its flesh to the city. The marble of Greece! It must be spoken of in terms of a substance which lives and changes according to mysterious laws. How else can one explain this snow whiteness overlaid with crystal powder and, next to it, this fawn patina?

The technique of the Greek artists, their method for capturing shadows in the columns' flutings, their delicate calculations for giving "ripeness" to an edifice and softening its severity—all this genius is obvious. But one could say that the block of marble understands their efforts and works secretly with them.

* * *

You must look, too, at the people, those in the country and those in the city. Don't hope to approach them easily. They are great lords receiving you.   When their ancestors were warring in the sun for their gods, ours were still living in dark forests.

They invented heroism and laid down the first laws which should govern a nation.   They invented physical prowess at the same time as mental discipline. We were still speaking onomato-poetically when they were discussing ideas.   Their sphinx was already speaking words.   Pythia was steeped in surrealism.   They founded the great relays towards which humanity will always strive.   Beauty, Liberty, Right, Justice are Greek words.   They capitalized them but used them easily.   They were members of the family.

They praised noble deeds and adored irony.   They revered their gods and heroes but could not resist riddling the first with arrows and banning the second.   Tragedy was born in the hiccoughs of their inebriety.   Ethics were in the hands of their immoralists.

* * *

The common people of Greece vary with each region.   Look closely at them and you will recall your ancient history.   Natives of Peloponnesus bear no resemblence to those of Thebes.   Between the shepherd of Elis and his Thessalian counterpart there is a striking contrast.   Rivalry between provinces died out over two thousand years ago but their ethnical purity is such that they survive in the gestures that welcome you and the looks that follow you.

Only the inhabitants of the Cyclades belong to the same family. It is a happier and more vivacious race than that of continental

Greece. Naxos, Myconos, Santorin may be more than mere ports of call so easy it is to discover the sweetness of life there. Everything is simple there but nothing is common. The people are comedians without knowing it. Young girls' eyes will be full of smiling ingenuousness but will give you to understand that a stranger could never be as handsome as a man of the islands. The fruit merchant will cheat you not out of cupidity but just for the fun of it. At Myconos, on my departure I gave a tie to the innkeeper's young son; he replied in sign language that he had already helped himself to one.

All these islands which are as old as the world will reveal to your eyes the dawn of life.

Crete, however, is an exception. Too many misfortunes, too many rivalries (since Pâris), and too many gods have invaded these mountains, caverns, and labyrinths for its people not to be haughty, suspicious and morose. Whom should one believe? Who is in command? The Minotaur, Zeus, Christ, the Pasha? One no longer knows.

The Cretan is unsociable, sleeps with his boots on, dresses his wife in black. He is a man on the alert. He is ready to revolt. During the last war, out of all these indolent islands where one lives in an operetta setting, Crete alone had an "operational theater." Swarms of Icaruses, wings outspread and knives open —that is what the Cretans saw in their sky. Peace returned, but not for long. A kidnapping scandal—still another!— broke out and divided the island into two clans. Crete's vocation is to go from one tragedy to another. Two novelists are well aware of this: Kazantzakis and Prevelakis.

Traveler, linger in front of the churches. Enter the monasteries. At the beginning, wild about columns and intoxicated by land-capes, I disdained them—but I was wrong. They are an essential part of Greece. The pope is the leader of the populace, as much among believers as the others. He takes part in their games and discussions. A person both familiar and venerated (and, on Mount Athos, as handsome as a bearded hermaphrodite), he steers his course through a sea passion like Ulysses among the reefs. On the islands—we had an excellent example of this at Cyprus—his power exceeds incense and ignites gunpowder.

On the outside a Byzantine chapel looks very much like a dovecote. The interior is often shabby. The gold is tarnished, the icon smoke-stained. Village worship for every heart. Occasionally, as in Daphni, a mosaic has survived. And one may see an image which has not been sugar-coated by the West. This is because the Pantocrator Christ sticks to the outposts. He must struggle not only against the Gentiles but also against the barbarian hordes. Hence his ferocious countenance. He is not supposed to charm but to frighten.

*　*　*

Lastly, look at the statues. You'll never have enough of them. Remind yourself that the Greek sculptor was the first to revolt against the established artistic style of monsters, grimacing gods and immobile forms. The body, only the human body, just as it is with its play of muscles and its slightest quivering—this is the result of his research and his vow of perfection. With the highest degree of skill and with the aid of a wet drapery he found it possible to retain its vital animation, even under a veil.

As the Athenian sculptor's eye descends his art becomes more elevated. Nike attaching her sandal is still more beautiful than when crying victory. In the Parthenon's frieze there is a certain voluntary negligence. There is nothing religious about the procession. The gestures are simple, disordered, hurried. Out of this scurry a new order of beauty was born in which naturalness, motion, and an instantaneous impression create the feeling.

All that man sees is beautiful if his eye is faithful—such is the teaching of the Greek sculptor before his models. This is the canon of Greek art.

This is even the sign of all Hellenic civilization. Springing from Nature, grounded in realism, it created nobility.

Jacques de LACRETELLE

So you are going to Greece! But which Greece do you expect to see?

For Greece is not just the country we know today, but rather a series of Greeces, each superimposed on the other like successive layers of soil recording the passage of time: Minoan and Mycenaean Greece; prehistoric, classical, Hellenistic, Greco-Roman, and Byzantine Greece; the Greece of the crusaders; Turkish and finally modern Greece.

Perhaps you will answer that you are not looking for any one of these many Greeces, but rather for all of them such as you can find at Lindos, a small town on the island of Rhodes, where ancient, medieval and the moribund modern closely overlap one another at the foot of a great, majestic acropolis.

More likely you will expect to find the mythical Greece—that fabulous and splendid Greece peopled with gods and heroes—whose memory we have cherished ever since our studies of Greek history and literature.

If it is true that we nurture the idea of a "real" Greece, born of half-learned lessons and of literary reminiscences, it is equally true that the Greece we find in the twentieth century resembles our preconception only faintly.

The expression "Eagles' Nest" applied to the Delphi region loses its emphatic character to become a humble statement of fact.

Each morning a few of these rare birds emerge from the rose-colored, prophetic mouths of the Phedriades rocks and take to the air like boats to the sea, cleaving the icy blue, transparent heights to fly over the ruins of the city of oracles and the cataract of sacred olive trees descending the Pleistos valley between Parnassus and Kirphis. By its color and sinuous course this cataract perpetuates the image of the Python serpent, guardian of this Chthonian fief, then called Pytho.

After the victory of Apollo Delphinus (the Cretan sailors' gay dolphin) over the brooding serpent, the name of the conquered territory was changed from Pytho to Delphi. Such a landscape is both a stage setting and a drama. The best definition of it is found in Rimbaud: a "fabulous opera."

Split in two like a honeycomb, this is the canal of Corinth. It permits ships of small tonnage to avoid going around Peloponnesus and provides direct communication between the Ionian and Aegean Seas. The crossing of it (which takes about twenty-five minutes) between two steep twin banks like the glacis of a fortress, is not without solemnity. This work which was carried out by a Franco-Hellenic company between 1882-1892, is ennobled, like emblazoned stationery, by a small niche topped by a triangular pediment hollowed out of the limestone during the days of the first works inaugurated by Nero with a gold shovel.

A steel bridge straddles the canal and carries trains or cars high enough to make them look like toys. A tame diversion preparing a transition during which the traveler's eye takes leave of one kind of light to discover another with all the required wonderment. For, on emerging from the canal into the Aegean Sea, the Greek miracle begins.

Even so, Greece cannot disappoint. She has never disappointed. The language she speaks is comprehensible to all ears.

A pure, almost unbearably brilliant light, illumines the magnificent, heart-rending truth that GREECE IS A LIVING BEING. Five centuries of hibernation under the Turks were unable to snuff out her breath of life dating back to antiquity. She is reborn each day, thus affirming that she is ever more exciting, ever more indispensable to our sensitivities; that she is a major element, an imperishable monument of our western civilization. By having her to start from, everything has become possible. Because of her, nothing is lost if mankind still knows what it means to see and to comprehend.

Since we may sometimes tend to forget, it is well to recall that Greece is peopled with Greeks—not just with mutilated statues—and that the Greek people have been endowed with exceptional qualities. The Greek miracle, which comes so often to mind as a moment of perfect civilization under Pericles, has never since renewed itself in architecture or in sculpture. This miracle has, however, left its impression on a race for whom invasions and occupations, though blurring its origins, have not been able to alter the stamp of its Greek soul.

I wish I could find the words to describe what I have felt in the company of Greeks. How poignant it is to discover in the middle of the twentieth century a people whose nobility and intelligence nothing has been able to alter! This nobility and this intelligence are inborn, and they remain always discreet, not revealing themselves until after an initial period of hesitation and reserve. The Greek must first be assured that the stranger (and everyone not born in the same village is a

Greece introduces itself at Corfu but a remnant of Italian alacrity subsists in the air. These two small isles and the canvas-covered boats which shuttle between them remind us of the Borromean Islands or those of the Venetian Lagoon.
Wlakhern shelters five or six nuns under the sloping roofs of a convent. Pondikonissi is more romanesque. Its cypress-circled rock speaks of Ulysses who was flung here by a storm, of Elizabeth of Austria who used to come here to consult a hermit, and of the painters Böcklin and Salvador Dali who made it the subject of famous paintings. Thus from Homer to the Surrealists this graceful basket of verdure placed on its marine tray has never failed to enchant imaginations.

Two decapitated lionesses mark the entrance to the Mycenaen menagerie where the show played to a full house. Behind this installation — resembling a prison more than a fortress — the wild beasts (*Atridae?* or *Perseids?*) licked themselves, tore each other apart, devoured each other, like one big happy family, but the burial of these carnivorous animals was carried out in great pomp. Blood and mud disappeared under a heap of gold. Today the dens of Mycenae or of Tyrinth have fallen into disuse but their original purpose cannot be forgotten. The fault lies with the dramatists (*Aeschylus, Sophocles, Euripides*), sorts of bluebottle flies attracted by the odor of charnel-houses.

stranger) is worthy of his friendship, that treasure which every man bears in the depths of his heart. Friendship as proffered by the Greek is immortal. It is transmitted from generation to generation. It renders meaningless all the differing circumstances of life. It abounds in generosity, becoming a sort of chef-d'œuvre. Even in its excesses—possessiveness and hypersensitivity— this friendship loves to seek sublimation.

Many tourists will visit Greece too quickly to be able to appreciate the secret of Greek friendship. What they will discover is kindness in everyone. However, although kindness is Mediterranean in scope, friendship, with its golden rule of hospitality, is a creation of Hellenic genius alone. To underestimate this is to miss the Greek people's great dream which has somehow managed to survive thirty centuries amid a world of hatred and discord. Although the word "xenophobia" is of Greek origin, its practice is unknown in the lands bordering the Ionian and the Aegean Seas. Whether Macedonian or Spartan, Athenian or Cretan, the Greek, despite his numerous regional differences, varies only in a few minor shortcomings, but never in his great qualities.

It is sad, on the other hand, to note the slow but unavoidable disappearance of all local color. Indeed, this phenomenon characterizes not only Greece but the rest of the world. We are rapidly moving toward a standardization of faces as well as of clothing.

Today we must accept Cretans without mustaches; and soldiers on the Greek frontiers wearing olive-drab instead of short, bouffant skirts.

We are shocked into sudden awareness of this standardization if, by chance, we happen to meet, on some out-of-the-way road in Greece, an old man handsomely clad in skirt and white stockings,

Here, vestiges and vegetation, far from distracting from each other, unite to compose a perfectly harmonious garden. The tall pines which accompany the Palestra columns in their skyward thrust were brought as seeds by a good wind from a neighboring hill without human intervention.

Wind of concord, faithful to the memory of the "sacred truces" which, every four years over an eight-century period, assembled all the people of Greece in common fervor for the corporal and mental perfection of their race.

Athen's expansion is contrary to the habitual trend of modern cities which develop towards the West. The wave of its new buildings abandons the Acropolis rock, center of the ancient city, passing by the Lycabettos, unfurling towards the more spacious East or North. In the daytime this plain of Attica where the city sprawls is like solidified sunlight. At night it becomes a mirror in which the starriest sky in the world is reflected. Athens is young for, in the words of Victor Hugo, it has triumphant mornings. The kiosk with its umbrella-shaped roof is called the Tower of the Winds but it is actually a marble clock which refuses to show any other time than the present instant. The street resembles that of a town in the Far West or Brasilia. And on the Acropolis, eternal youth center dominating all the rest, those are not broken temples which we see but simply unfinished ones.

riding on horseback or walking toward us with assured steps; or a Cretan wearing suspenders, red belt and black boots; or a peasant woman from Empona on the island of Rhodes, dressed in embroidery of gold, red and black, and wearing heavy, fawn-colored boots; or a tiny married woman from Metsovon in Epirus, seated on her pony like an Amazone, her large, embroidered skirt spread out and revealing white-stockinged ankles; or at the gate of the Royal Palace, on Syntagma Place in Athens, the last of the Evzones —these tall guardians of the federal power— handsome as toy-soldiers. It takes no effort at all to imagine the sort of nineteenth century Greek familiar to Chateaubriand, Byron, Gobineau and Edmond About.

Greece, having won the liberation of her homeland as far as what might be called its natural limits (although every Greek still has yearnings toward Istanbul which his heart will always call "Constantinople"), has shaken off a heavy load of traditions which were carefully maintained as a defiance to her occupier. Greeks have now learned to read and write, whereas formerly, by means of illiteracy, they protected themselves against Turkish education. However, they preserve with sacred respect certain religious customs whose archaism is touching because it keeps alive pagan ceremonies of the past within the context of present, popular religion.

One of the first questions every visitor to Greece asks himself, now as in the past, is: How did such a country as Greece ever come about? How has it been able to enjoy an exceptional civilization for twenty-five centuries? How did Greece manage to dominate the Mediterranean? How was she finally conquered? How has she been able to impregnate the Occident to such a degree that

Temple of an active, hardworking parish of gunsmiths, blacksmiths and potters, the temple of Theseus is not Theseus' sanctuary but that of Athena Hephaestus, patron of the industrial arts. As blond as the Parthenon (its scarcely younger brother) and hewed out of the same Pentelican marble, this edifice is nonetheless a "minor," interesting rather than exalting. Its merit lies in having preceeded with talent the flowering of genius. It is an excellent teacher of style, thanks to its state of conservation. Architectural students the world over are diligent in studying it and praising, with reason, its somewhat stiff elegance and exemplary uprightness. Can such dignified manners explain the whim which, at the beginning of the nineteenth century, made the Theseus the necropolis of English Protestants?

Could anyone doubt, on contemplating the Acropolis sheep on the left and the Corinthian ones on the right, that all of them belong to the same flock? Curiously, the light caught by the photographic objective brings out the same relief on marble and on wool. Another occasion to admire the skill of Greek sculptors and their faithfulness to reality...

... But the little Corinthian shepherd loves his animals too much not to turn them away from the glorious road leading straight to the sacrifice. The crook with which he tries to keep them in peaceful pastures is an accessory whose origin would be lost in the night of time if time were not only an illusion in Greece. It is a "glizza," the hook of which resembles the venemous serpents whose bite is averted by peircing them with a stick. The nail attaching the hook to the cane represents the reptile's eye and the glizza is almost always made of olivewood.

even now philosophers refer to Aristotle, doctors to Aesculapius, playwrights to Aeschylus, poets to Homer, historians to Thucydides?

Geopolitics, although not pretending to be able to explain everything, is, nonetheless, able to account for a great deal. What cannot be explained, however, must be left to chance or, perhaps, to those gods who both blessed Greece and then ground her down; to those gods who inspired men and then punished them for their justifiable pride.

To the traveler on his first visit to Greece, poverty is a predominant feature. Although I have no intention to plead the case for poverty, we would do well to remember the following: nowadays, poverty, kept at bay with a battery of refrigerators, television sets and washing machines, appears to us only as a regrettable blemish. But there was a time in history when poverty exalted the virtues and goaded finer minds to resolve problems which menaced man's destiny. Poverty did, indeed, shape the face of ancient Greece, but it was accompanied by the radiance of an inner splendor.

What can be more revealing in this respect than the road leading from Athens to Cape Sounion? After passing several well-known beaches and newly-planted pine-groves, the road runs alongside a rusty-gray cliff. Here there is not a tree or bush to be found; only here and there a clump of nettles. On the right hand lies the sea, wide and blue—the Saronic Gulf—as well as the first of the Cyclades and a few dead, bare, tiny islands crowned with a white chapel. Nothing can, in fact, seem as desolate as this. One's eye does not fix on anything but wanders until it is arrested by the sight of the temple of Poseidon standing against the sky and glistening in the sun.

In the shade of Olympia, weddings of vegetable and mineral are often celebrated. Here is the announcement of one of these blissful marriages: that of the hollyhock and the column.

Situated at the extreme end of Attica, the Cape of Sounion seems to stand watch over all of Greece. Under a low, gray sky this would be an even more desolate country, but the sky arches high above, the wind has chased away all remaining clouds, and the sea is flecked with white foamcrests.

Irresistibly the mind's eye sketches on the horizon the great Asiatic fleet of Xerxes: twelve hundred ships filled with men and arms. What could these mercenaries from the Orient have thought of their commanders upon this first glimpse of Greece? They had been promised a land of fabulous treasure, a land whose name was supreme throughout the Mediterranean, and now, at their approach to it, they could see nothing appearing but bare rock. For everyone among them who was aware of the greatness of Greece, there were many who must have felt chagrin at its harshness and poverty. "What? Is this all that Greece amounts to!"

Signs of life were just as rare then as now. Only on those small bays where they were protected from the winds did fisherfolk live, and only when some small valley offered shade and water did farmers gather together to plant orchards, olive-groves and a little wheat. The very lay-out of this peninsula had made it into many little communities independent of one another—societies accustomed to depend on themselves for a living; to defend themselves without outside help; to form their politics according to the most diversified principles; and to establish their particular code of morals.

Life was frugal for them in those times and it has remained so throughout the centuries. The Greeks could offer only the slenderest of satisfactions to the covetous Orientals. These potential invaders saw, of course, the temple of Poseidon

Mykonos' originality is to have no history. Its dazzling houses, its terraces more beautiful than those of Algiers, its beach and, above all, the fat cheerfulness of its windmills, create a setting which reminds us of both St. Tropez and the Dutch countryside. Besides, it is the island of painters, along with Hydra. The Greek government arranged for low-rent studios there, thus founding a village of artists more unconstrained and alive than the formal French Villa Medicis in Rome. The familiar, everyday charm of this Cyclade makes one forget that it was the port of embarkation for Delos, the harshest of the islands, cradle of the harshest of the gods: Apollo, Artemis; and where the wind (blowing from December to December) snatches bald all who linger there. Foreigners, of course.

The sanctuary of Athena Lindia on the Lindos acropolis was much in vogue during the Hellenic era. Its admirers came not only from Greece but Egypt and Macedonia as well, and even from Crimea. Today, from the look of these white uniforms, they come from even more distant points to photograph the remaining elements (reinforced with new, somewhat flashy material) which give an idea of the Lindian civilization at its zenith.

This handsome group of stairways, terraces, and Doric columns is rather ostentatious.

It may be that its builders, attentive like all Greek architects to the landscape's counsel, received from that of Lindos, which is more intense than subtle, an invitation to lay it on thick.

perched audaciously above the sea when they drew closer to land, but then, who sets out with twelve hundred ships to pillage a temple? Xerxes did not cheat his men, however; the Hellenes lived frugally from the fruits of nature but opulently indeed from the riches they created by their talent, taste and intelligence. For them, the simpler life was, the more fervently they turned toward superior satisfactions : architecture, sculpture and the exchange of knowledge. This tiny country, which belonged neither to Europe nor to the Middle East, possessed a great secret.

One can attribute this secret partly to the sterility of the soil upon which the first Greeks lived. An imaginative life, not dissipating itself in pleasure-pursuits, turns to other aspirations. The Greek, living from day to day on wheat, cheese and olive-oil, enjoyed mutton, fish and strong Peloponnesian wine only on festival days. The menu of the modern Greek has scarcely changed at all, and he never tires, whether in an inn or at home, of the same dishes: roast mutton, cucumber salad, white cheese, apples or oranges. He has never seen fit to vary his wines and is quite unconcerned if nothing so resembles a resinous wine as another resinous wine. On the other hand, he is a great connoisseur of spring-water. It is in Greece that foreigners take on what is often a new habit to them, of drinking water before each meal. This habit is, naturally, more closely observed in summer in this arid country than in winter. So highly esteemed is water that the serving of a glass of spring-water has long been the first compliment paid to a guest. This custom seems to symbolize all the simplicity that is Greece.

Born to a frugal way of life, the Greek has always lived outdoors. Although women are still after three thousand years confined to their homes,

At *Mykonos, island of windmills, the houses, chapels, and stairways or, in other words, the stone, marble and quicklime rival each other in whiteness. The stage seems to be set for the entrance of a chorus of flour-merchants singing Offenbach's well-known refrain:*
"For the flour-merchants are all white, all white
All white, all white, etc..."

ΤΑΒΕΡΝΑ
ΙΩΑΝ. Α. ΛΙΟΥΛΗ

I*t was the Gree*
whitewashed hous
For isn't the imp
the classic sheep

nted the admirable adage: "Not too much of anything." This indifference to luxury and ornamentation explains the ageless elegance of their
aw-bottomed chairs and unpainted tables assembled under the porches of cafés and out in the country in the shade of olive trees and tamarisks.
g to dwell among friends? And this friendship would not be complete if it were limited to human intercourse. Animals play a role too, from
iting the special treat of a pinch of tobacco from his shepherd to the unusual pelican mascot who has become Mykonos' citizen of honor.

their husbands as well as young unmarried men are always to be found, when not at work, in cafés and other public places. In ancient times this practice was tantamount to public duty. Today it no longer has this function—even though public life is still effervescent—but has become a custom and, I was about to say, a vice. The Greek loves to loiter about. He does not measure time as we do, and the weather, conveniently for him, encourages this attitude.

Winters (except in Salonika and the mountains) are mild, and autumn is magnificent. Only in springtime is the weather capricious: southerly winds encounter those from the north, the sea becomes rough, and rain falls as a final mercy before the summer sun scorches the countryside.

Spring remains, however, a favored time of the year. The islands and the continent are covered with wild flowers: poppies and yellow and white daisies. An endless sweet fragrance covers the whole of this ungenerous soil and lasts as long as the roses. Three hot days are enough to scorch the wheat and dry out the earth. Once again Greece becomes gray and straw-yellow, a color which, when seen from a distance, melts by some unknown alchemy into ineffable somber-purples and velvet-blues.

Placed in the midst of this magnificent setting devoid of artifice, the Greek remains in direct communion with beauty. The roughest goatherd, isolated on the solitary heights of Parnassus or Olympus, finds the right words to celebrate the grandeur which surrounds him and the right words to express his own dreams, visions and ideals.

The stranger, disembarking at Piraeus and seeing Athens for the first time, may well have doubts about these initial observations. These

The Greek architect is a discoverer by the same right as the man who makes a treasure spring from the earth. At the end of the fourth century the man who was responsible for the Epidaurus theater, Polyclitus the Younger, on a territory sanctified by the presence of the god of medicine, proceeded to a sort of delivery which had as much to do with obstetrics as with architecture.

Thanks to his obstetrical attentions, the Kynortion Mountain gave birth to a human masterpiece which presents itself to the world as a natural wonder. (Whorls of shells or calcareous rock eroded by water?) The theater of Epidaurus deserted is, to me, the best show. However, not everyone would agree with me. The "festival-goers" have restored its functional character. Every year more or less authorized voices benefit from its famous accoustics. It's only fair, after all, that such a gigantic oyster should again attract seekers of pearls.

two cities—really forming one—overcrowded, suffocating, awkward and often hideous, are as far removed as possible from the image we have cherished of Greece. The extremely rapid growth of these two agglomerations (containing one and a half million inhabitants out of a total of 8,000,000 for all of Greece) has occurred with depressing disorder.

The modern Greek has lost all sense of urbanism. His architects construct slipshod, modern districts of unbelievable ugliness. Patras, Larissa, Kalamai, the new Corinth and Heraklion are cities of a hideousness which defies reason. These towns give the impression that they are only temporary, as if they had been put up in great haste in the secret hope that they would be swept away by time, and that the citizens could then return to the archaic and rustic life of the Ancients—that is, to the only life which could give man the right to fritter away his time, to taste life to the full. Can it perhaps be that, since the countryside is so intensely beautiful, a man having to leave it even temporarily, abandons all will to fight against ugliness? Greek cities are, almost without exception, great disappointments. The most one can wish is that they will somehow manage to make themselves forgotten like Sparta, Olympia or Volos. For every Návpaktos, Pilos or Methoni, there are, unhappily, all too many cities like Missolonghi, Itea and Tripolis.

But why not forget these cities? In Greece they are only accidents anyway. Perhaps after acquiring a patina of age, they will one day crack, disintegrate, and end up by reverting to the countryside. The end-product of this process may still be observed in places like Epidaurus, Delphi, Olympia, or on the Athenian Acropolis.

To achieve the revelation of Epidaurus takes

At Delphi, high spot of religion, every Greek city was represented by a chapel destined to proclaim its glory. Around 535, the inhabitants of Siphnos, on learning that their island was a goldmine, hastened to thank Apollo with a temple where the vigorous Ionian art flourished. This art, born in Eastern Greece, dominated the entire archaic period, accompanying the Hellenes right to Sicily. Its simple grandeur, its animation and concern for realistic details confer on the Homeric episodes chosen by the sculptors of this treasure the same documentary importance as the tapestries of Bayeux for the period of William the Conqueror. But in this case, the artists' incredible mastery, their knowledge of the powers of reliefs and line and even their stubborn habit of putting full-face eyes in profiles, engender a sort of "perpetual melody," the true plastic correspondence with the magic of Wagner.

Man's reverie, determination or vanity sometimes leave their mark on earth. But in the sea they dissolve leaving no trace. On the feverish water of the Missolonghi lagoon can this fisherman be remembering Byron? The cab, the bicycle and the peaceful strollers on the Preveza quay are skirting with nary a shiver a body of water on which Octavius and Antony's partisans fought, where the fight of Cleopatra's galley changed the face of the world. These steamers at anchor in the Piraeus accentuate its resemblance with Le Havre or Rotterdam. Perhaps only this Corfiote boatman remembers Homer because his parents named him Ulysses and because his fiancée, Nausicaa the laundress, has promised to meet him on the quiet shores of the Pondikonissi island.

only a few minutes: the time necessary to climb up the tiers and to seat oneself high in the back of the amphitheater. To arrive at this amphitheater one crosses a wide valley, passes by temple-ruins and the weed-covered remains of a stadium. Suddenly one finds oneself on the stage of the theater, facing empty rows. The finest actor in the world would have stage-fright. Surely the visitor is entitled to feel the same discomfort. He can test the acoustic properties and clap his hands. Something is still missing. But just let him climb the steps of rose and white limestone; his reward and revelation will be found once he has arrived at the top. From this vantage-point the visitor sees how the whole setting falls into place; how the mountain-backdrop forms its own amphitheater, with the sky at just the right height. In the afternoon the sun shone over the backs of 14,000 spectators on to the front of the actors on stage, lighting up their faces and bathing the valley-landscape in an oblique illumination. Only a genius could have conceived and built this faultless arrangement.

From the top tier is revealed one of the finest panoramas in the world. The eye does not butt up against the mountains themselves, but sketches slowly and thoughtfully the silhouette from mountain-crest to mountain-crest. One has the feeling that one has only to stretch out the arms to touch these hills—the breasts of Hera—in order to feel their gray-green, muted against the sky. Nothing here oppresses by its weight. Everything is feather-light. It seems as if the least wind could give imaginary wings to these summits of daring design.

How can one keep one's thoughts from drifting toward this manifestation of Greek pride? From the topmost tier down to the circular stage it is evident how all has been conceived in order that

Among the traditional holidays inscribed on the Greek calendar, Easter has no equal in brilliance: religious services, open-air meals, folklore dances, military reviews. The pappas' chasubles, the peasant dress and military uniforms make up gaudy flowerbeds which compete in color with the first flora of Spring. The costumes of the evzones (a sort of honor guard) would require, in order to be depicted according to their merits, Delacroix's palette for the jacket and that of Degas for the bouffant skirt. Once the first astonishment has worn off, this dress awakens the most noble memories. The white wool stockings model the evzones' legs like those of statues and their skirts are pleated like fluted columns. The large pompoms on their slippers pointing up like the prow of a felucca perpetuate Achilles' light step or the young Sophocles' dance after the victory of Salamis. Wasn't it the ponderous Nietzsche who wrote:
"The hero is lighthearted and dances in battle."

man may dominate and encompass man: indeed, the freedom of the actor is defined within the limits of the marble-backed seats and the open sky. But these limits which man imposed upon himself do not apply to the work of the gods. The theater of Epidaurus, cut in porphyry whose rose-tones are heightened by the setting sun, looks out over a changeless land-scape which nothing seems to have marred throughout the centuries.

If Epidaurus is a slow revelation, the Acropolis of Athens is a shock so violent as to have remained for twenty-five centuries a source of unremitting wonder and admiration to civilized people. On this miniature mountain, set like a tombstone in the heart of Athens, man has once and for all come near to God. Here man's approach to God —unlike that of the preposterous builders of the tower of Babel or that of the pharaohs and their pyramids whose egocentrism crushed the ambition of a whole people—was that of a meditation forceful enough to assume shape, to inscribe itself in a framework of stone. The human and the divine, here united as they had never been before, nor ever again would be, achieve a heart-filling harmony. The Acropolis is, indeed, the center of the world. Standing on its terrace, one's thoughts turn successively to Orient and Occident—united in, then liberated from the baroque only to aspire, thereupon, to nothing more than further spoliation.

A fragment of Baudelaire's verse comes to mind: "There, all is simply order and beauty." One's eye strays toward the Saronic Gulf, caresses the Hymettus mountain, slides up the long slope of Lycabettus, flies above Kitissia, re-climbs the Sacred Way, and perceives in the distance the Bay of Eleusis, this time devoid of its mysteries. At the foot of the rock spreads out a white Athens whose breath is a cloud of light dust at roof-top

Mykonos has completely forgotten that it once served as a graveyard for the giants slain by Herakles. Yet the natives here have a reputation for liking tales and are not above composing a few tall ones themselves, which relates them to Alphonse Daudet's peasants in Southern France. The homely flavor of such a landscape is not only restful but instructive as well: the position of this very human island which is the port of embarkation for Delos, fief of implacable gods, seems to designate the exact position where man should place himself in relation to divine perfection. Heedless of Olympian quarrels and taking the wind as it comes, the miller of Mykonos, on the threshold of his mill, fills his pipe.

level. The gray fumes of Piraeus add an impressionistic note to this vast, unique panorama.

We should reflect for a moment: Against this sepulchral rock ten... a hundred attacks were repulsed. Then came the hundred first, and all the others which followed... The fact that it remained intact until 1687, when the cannon-ball of the Doge Morosini blew it to pieces, is no less astonishing. Just a year earlier, in 1686, Gravier d'Olières and several French officers examined the monuments of the Acropolis and made sketches of them. These sketches offer the most complete idea of what remained at that time. Three centuries later, it must be left to the imagination to reconstitute the whole from the few remaining columns, the two pediments and the pieces of frieze assembled together in the most perfect little museum in the world. Here the power of the past is so strong that it is possible to say: nothing is lacking. Genius in the form of the "indwelling spirit of place" has won a victory over stupidity, savagery and incomprehension.

The incantatory power of Delphi is different. This time the countryside is no longer dominated, organized and classified by the Greek. Here, it is as though the temples and the stadium had been embedded in the flank of the mountain in order to cling to the grandiose tragedy of the cliffs of Phaedriades and the slopes of Parnassus. Nature here was too rich and overpowering. It was necessary to yield to it, to form a union with it, to build massively (the columns of the temple of Apollo are more than two yards in diameter) without hope of ever fighting against the crushing mass of Parnassus. Seen from the other side of the gorge of Pleistos, Delphi is no longer distinguishable except as an ant-heap in a vast ensemble of chaotic nature.

Between the steep sides of the rock cliffs flows

Emperor of solitude, musician of silence, the temple of Bassae provokes in the soul of every visitor, even the forewarned, that sort of moral earthquake engendered by phenomena of a supernatural order. Thus, we can easily imagine the emotion of the French architect Bocher when, in 1764, he accidentally discovered this gem in its lofty Arcadian hiding place. Situated at 4,000 feet on the edge of a gullied plateau overlooked by the grim peaks of the Ithoma, Lyceum and Taygetus mountains, the temple of Bassae was dedicated in the years 420-415 B.C., by the Phigalians to Apollo who had saved them from the plague. The work was entrusted to Ictinos, architect of the Parthenon. Ictinos was up to his par and yet without repeating himself. Bassae, which is less ambitious than its twenty-year elder (38 meters by 14: the Parthenon 69 meters by 30) tempers the austerity of the Doric by the grace of the Ionian and even permits the flowering of a Corinthian column, the only one of its order and the first in a Greek temple. In spite of the loss of its pediments, this masterpiece is the best conserved of all Greek sanctuaries, along with the Theseus of Athens.

"Tranquil columns crowned
With the adornments of day,"
Without a doubt, this distich by
Valéry addresses itself to the picture on the left. But what about this
one?
"Our antique youths
Mat flesh and beautiful shadows."
Doesn't it refer to the image on
the right?
In the country of metamorphoses
and fables nothing could arrest what
Malebranche calls "the volubility
of our mind." Is the column an alibi
for a woman? The caryatid a stand-
in for a column? And even if we
refer to the tradition (a questionable
one) which has the marble column
descend from the tree trunk supporting the roof of the primitive
hut, the mystery is still complete.
Tree and goddess are so inseparable
that another French poet, Ronsard,
tried to restrain the woodcutter's
arm in the Gastine Forest, crying,
"See you not the scarlet droplets
swell
From nymphs residing under its
tough shell?"

The temple of Athena Nike appears
to have been built in the image of one of
those light cages in which pious Greeks
enclosed and carried doves to sacrifice. It
is boldly placed on the brink of the sacred
cliff on which Aegeus anxiously awaited
the appearance of the white sail in the
Saronic Gulf by which his son Theseus was
to announce his victory over the Minotaur.
Accidentally (or through a desire to reign)
Theseus hoisted a black sail and Aegeus
threw himself over the cliff.
The Victories are far too capricious lady-
birds for the Greeks not to have tried to
capture at least one of them. Having chosen
her, they cut her wings and crowned her
with Athena's helmet. Then they built
this marble cage for her with ionic columns,
its prison-like appearance reinforced in
ancient times by bronze bars blocking the
two lateral bays and going right up to the
capitals. The cage was so beautiful and
the exposure so pleasant that it acted upon
the free Victories like a mirror on a lark,
transforming the balustrade along the
Pyrgos crest into a dove-cote of superb
girls with beating wings.
Having literally lost their heads, these
scatterbrains have become jailbirds. Their
still quivering remains may be admired in
a room in the Acropolis Museum.

an Amazon of olive trees which broadens to a delta until it reaches the Corinthian Sea at Itea. We know from history all that Delphi signified in the life of ancient Greece, but history becomes insignifiant when such a panorama unrolls before the eyes. Nothing is wanting here—not even the eagles of tragedy whose soaring flights in the upper air described strange arabesques, upon which were based interpretations of oracular utterances. For centuries a whole people used to come here to learn their destiny and to pray to the local protecting spirits. Later, after the oracle replied with an earthquake—knocking down temples, altars, statues, and burying treasures—only the statue of the charioteer emerged, bearing his marvelous expression of wonderment.

The Delphi museum contrains the essential manifestations of Greek devotional art. Bigotry is completely lacking. This religious art is solidly virile and, with regard to the goddesses and nymphs, of a moving tenderness. Because the Greeks of Delphi talked to their gods in one of the most terrifying sites in the world, they vied in candor, virtue and humility.

If it is at Epidaurus, on the Athenian Acropolis, and at Delphi where the "indwelling spirit of place" is most overwhelming, this same spirit is also manifest elsewhere, sometimes with grace and calm, sometimes with great majesty. At every encounter it imposes an idea of ancient Greece so complete that it seems to embrace everything at one time.

I should have preferred to eliminate from these pages all advice and all reference to itineraries. A trip to Greece is a personal adventure, where the presence of an outsider runs the risk of adding confusion. It is essential to be alone to have the illusion of inventing a Greece for oneself.

Situated at the crossroads of sea routes leading from Europe to Asia or Africa, home of the Minotaur, of the painter called El Greco, and of Venizelos, here is Crete — Minoan at Knossos or at Phaestos, Venetian at the ports of Candia or of Canea, Provençal in the valley of Malea and the only Greek country where one has dared to speak of the death of the God of gods.

It would require much time and knowledge to decipher its enigmatic countenance. Archeologists are still disputing the reasons for the flowering of such a civilization during the Bronze Age, for its interruption and then resumption around 1700 B.C. and its destruction around 1400 B.C. Although the showcases of Cretan museums are chock full of delicate marvels the ruins of palaces remain a dead letter for me. They are labyrinths in which I haven't the slightest desire to get lost. I know that Ariadne is no longer there to guide me with a thread. Theseus' "fatal fickleness" led her to Naxos. There she drowned her sorrow in the charming arms of the god of the vine.

I shall therefore leave the tourist to climb alone Mount Cynthus on Delos. Here he will experience a new feeling: at his feet spreads out a sanctuary where statues have been mutilated, columns broken, and a theater gutted by some stupid fury at one time or another. But this fury cannot prevent the eye from ignoring the disaster and instead, appreciating with emotion the plan of the dead city, its avenues, its little streets, its agora, the sacred lake, the esplanade and an ancient quay. There is no one here except the guardians, wearing peaked caps. One must ask their permission to visit the dwelling of Dionysius and that of Poseidon.

It is really from Mount Cynthus that one must contemplate Delos—this little lost island of the Cyclades, battered continually by rough seas churned by the wind of the "melthemi." Here the setting is brilliant royal blue beneath a pale sky. There is not a tree to divert one's attention. Delos resembles the carapace of a turtle cropping out of the surface of water. The horizons are studded with the islands of Mykonos, Tinos, Syros, Paros and Naxos—sometimes straw-colored, sometimes purple in the rays of the setting sun, or, at other times, altogether lost in the haze born of heat or spray. In no other part do the Cyclades afford so much seduction to the dreamer fond of myths. These islands reaffirm all that is audacious in the Greek.

On this sea which Homer described as "winy," frail craft have transported tons and tons of marble and thousands of pilgrims. The trip is still rough aboard the caiques which ply in the morning between Mykonos and Delos. The craft bobs like a cork on the foamy waves. Nature was not kind to man here, but man has succeeded in overcoming nature.

Of the indolent Corinth, one of the richest and most teeming cities of the ancient Mediterranean, whose devotion to the "Venus of nocturnal love" (Venus Melania) nimbed it in a somewhat tarnished glory, the irony of fate decreed that there would remain standing, victorious over time, invasion and earthquakes, only seven columns of the severest style. These venerable survivors date from the first half of the eleventh century. They belong to a Doric temple dedicated to Apollo. The contour of their monolithic shafts, the swelling echinus of their capitals have a coarse vigor which undoubtedly explains their resistance.

Until its decline Corinth fought tooth and nail to thwart all attempts to divide the isthmus which was its fortune. Since the opening of the canal the modern port of Nea Korinthos has vegetated. But the heath which replaced the city which was too mercantile-minded to ever have given birth to an artist of worth, is carpeted each spring with wild flowers whose colors seem to be reflected in the stone of the old columns. An instant of pardon which the camera was able to record.

The bare and arid Cyclades, where white cubes of villages nestle in the shelter of infrequent harbors, have defied three thousand years of piracy, invasions and neglect.

Even more impressive is the fact that these islands remained, during a whole epoch, more alive than Greece itself because the mainland was occupied by the Turks. It was from Hydra and Spetsai that warships sailed during the nineteenth century to liberate the mother country. Down to the moment of its overthrow in 1824, Psara was one of the last bastions of independence. While the Greek mainland was living in misery, many islands prospered: they had command of the sea, and the sea was, for them, liberty.

It is with a certain melancholy that one rediscovers these dead glories today. Whereas many islands were formerly rich and powerful, they were ruined when the mother country regained independence. Indeed, many would have collapsed altogether were it not for tourism's imbuing them with the new life-blood of a profitable industry.

Such, for example, is the case of the delightful Dodecanese island of Castelorizo whose name is derived from the Frankish knights: "Château-Roux." Another typical case is that of Patmos whose spiritual influence formerly extended throughout the whole of the middle East. Today this island owes its existence to visiting cruise-ships.

Here there is scope for some melancholy reflections on the ebb and flow of life.

Louis Jouvet gave the name of "minute théâtrale" to that momentary fusion of text, actor and audience in a single emotion—an emotion so unique as to be necessarily fleeting. During this experience our heart curbs its beating and the ineffable captures our soul.

Saint Irene to whom Santorin owes its name (through a deformation of the Venetian Santa Irini) has poorly protected her namesake. The unhappy fate of this Cyclade is to serve as a battlefield for armies from Heaven and Hell, the latter embodied in a volcano of which Santorin is one of the vertiginous inner sides, while the submerged crater occupies the center of the roadstead. The volcano's activity modifies the landscape causing islets to appear or disappear. Very recently the white village of Thira which brightened the summit of the cinder-colored cliff was ravaged by a terrible eruption. But a zigzagging ramp still laces the steep hill which must be climbed to go from the port to the village. Aside from three trees: a palm and two pines, the island's vegetation is reduced to vines which produce in periods of calm a muscat wine whose bouquet is somewhat like the famous Lacryma-Christi, growing at the foot of Vesuvius.

The joy of living in Greece has only one explanation: the friendliness of its people. It is not polite kindness but heartfelt, full of absolute confidence. To be permitted to take part in the daily life of these artisans and merchants whose customs have remained unchanged since Homer's day, is to partake of the magic leaven which insures the eternal youth of the gods. On the small squares fanned by pepper trees or in the alvioli which serve as shops the Greek people move about, chat, prove the vitality of a race which no invasion, no historical event has been able to deform, crush or keep from thriving. A marvelous demonstration of equilibrium and wisdom, of respect for others through self-respect.

What on earth was the purpose of this Tholos, a charming rotunda erected on the site called Marmaria, the first station of the Delphian pilgrimage if one follows Pausanias' itinerary? A work of Attic style in white Pentelican marble with a plain moulding of Eleusinian blue limestone, the Tholos today appears to have known no other destiny than that of accentuating by its immobile waltz the general plan of the landscape which is to revolve. The petrified gyration of the rocks, the mountains, the bay of Itea, the round of sacred olive trees encourage the delirium of the Pythia of Delphi on her tripod. The Oracle obeyed the impulsion of the setting like a record on a phonograph. Apollo dug into her flesh with his hard sapphire, delivering her oraculous music.

The Greek countryside affords so many of these "theatrical moments" that even a lengthy enumeration would not be exhaustive. The photographer's joy is to be able to capture these fleeting moments, to "snap" them, and to preserve them as an aid to memory which fails under the weight and variety of so many disparate images.

No one should miss a cloudy day at the temple of Bassae in the heart of an Arcadia no longer Olympian but ever savage and red and black—an Arcadia punctuated by occasional Judas trees among oaks and rocks. Bassae, in its morose solitude at the summit of a hill which one climbs by a strenuous route, surges out of the past like an admirably tattered phantom. Discovered only two centuries ago in a region where there were not even any shepherds, the temple had resisted the ravages of wind and cold for 2,200 years. But it proved to be less resistant to the archæologists.

The stripped walls and the bare pediment have lost their sculpture—together with the plaques of the frieze and the metopes—to the British Museum along with the rest of the spoils of Lord Elgin. At Bassae I indulged in the hope that in a great gesture of solidarity and generosity, Great Britain, Germany, and France—the three countries which have most "relieved" Greece of its sculptures— would get together and agree to return the masterpieces to their original sites. What an idle dream! In her distress it was often Greece herself who sold the purest treasures of her past in order to finance her struggle against the Turks. Bassae will never again find her glory intact, as did the archæologist Bocher who discovered it quite by chance during an excursion in 1765. What sloth and ignorance had preserved, curiosity and the greed of museums destroyed! What remains overwhelms with beauty and strength. Frequent clouds,

For the entertainment of a nice sailor audience, the Acropolis, under the bright lighting of a super-production, tells the story of its life.

For the take-it-with-you education of the "Metics" (all non-Athenians) smitten by beauty to the point of exhaustion, gods, godesses, temples and philosophers are sold in all sizes and shapes in a wide range of prices. This system of popularizing culture is not without risk. History quickly turns to anecdote and sculpture to soapcarving.

drawn on and chased away by the wind, alternately hide and reveal this temple, abandoned to its solitary existence.

The palace of Minos at Phaestos (Crete) offers a "theatrical moment" no less grandiose. This time the imagination must take a leap backward some five millenia to re-create this fabulous palace erected upon a burial ground overlooking the russet-and-gold, sun-scalded plain of the valley of Mesara. Here beat the heart of a strong and ingenious civilization whose games spread to the four corners of the Mediterranean. Here, too, was a unique example of a peaceful civilization which scorned war and did not surround itself with walled fortifications. Archæologists are still trying to ascertain what scattered the Minoan civilization to the winds of the centuries: invasion, plague or earthquake. Perhaps it would be charitable to allocate to each factor its due share by suggesting that it need not necessarily have been barbarism or plague, but simply that invincible enemy of man: Time.

In Crete, Valéry's frightening pronouncement about the death of civilizations acquires an aspect of bitterness. An all-pervading and seemingly blind justice metes out, with a stinting hand, to certain Cretans the right to emerge from the chaos. Crete knew several centuries of perfection followed by silence and suffering. When seen from the burial ground of Phaestos, Crete now appears to be peaceful and beautiful beneath its cloudy sky. Liberty, rediscovered, has dressed its wounds.

But what terrible suffering in order to arrive at this peace! Towns and cities as well as men and women still bear traces of this suffering. In the history of martyrs, Crete has its own special chapter: fires, tortures, deportations, reprisals, crucifixions, massacres and devastations. Out of this

The setting sun covers the arrid flanks of Mount Hymettus in a tunic of flowers, then in a tunic of gems which are just so many mirages. On the spot and even in the springtime, reality is more austere. (Monsieur Renan wrote: "It could be that the truth is sad.") Heather has replaced the profusion of aromatic plants of ancient times and the bees, dispensers of the famous honey, have emigrated to Mount Pentelicus. But in this vertical desert Kaisariani is an oasis full of unassuming charm.
A former monastery like Daphni (today a state-owned farm) Kaisariani proposes a delicate stage-setting for reverie. It includes a small church, the oldest sections of which go back to the ninth century, a cloister, antique vestiges restored with taste, cypress-trees, and a spring whose water was greatly appreciated by Athenians. It was sold, like a famous vintage, in small casks wrapped in leaves.
The Kaisariani landscape, like its spring, is a swallow of freshness for parched eyes.

suffering has been born a race of men tempered by misfortune and resolute determination. Even now, high on the snow-covered slopes of Mount Ida, live clans in villages accessible only by mule-back. Their customs would fascinate those ethnologists not wholly preoccupied with trying to predict the world's future among the Bantu or the Indians of the Amazon.

No matter how numerous his particular traits, the Cretan remains, nonetheless, Greek. Through the centuries his obstinacy to reunite with his lost mother country reaches the point of absurdity. This urge arises from the depths of his heart where he recognizes his virtues as being those of the Greeks of Attica, of Peloponnesus, or of Macedonia. The first of these virtues is always friendship, the sacred duty of hospitality. The entire island looks toward Europe, turning its back on nearby Africa whose hot winds ripen Cretan wheat at the onset of spring. The Cretan's longing is purely sentimental because Greece is self-sufficient. In Mediterranean history, Greece could have gone her own way, independent and disdainful.

Like Phaestus, the palaces of Mallia and Hagia Triada, the dead city of Gortyna and the precious relics of the museum of Heracleum — all these bear witness to such a prodigious advance over the rest of contemporary humanity as to be inevitably fatal to their audacious creators.

Modern Crete shows little concern over these ancient souvenirs. It was the English (particularly, the very curious and fantasy-ridden Sir Arthur Evans) at Knossos; the Italians at Phaestus and Hagia Triada; the French at Mallia; and the Americans at Gortyna, who excavated and revealed the Minoan civilization. The Cretan, however, lives in the present. This is partly out of a sense

Fort Bourzi which is a Venetian building should not feel in exile in the Bay of Nauplia where the water mirror reflects the hues of the setting sun as at Venice in the dead lagoon between Murano and Torcello.
A jetty formerly joined the island to the land. Present-day tourism has made a palace of this edifice which was long the home of executioners whom the Greek people superstitiously kept at a certain distance.

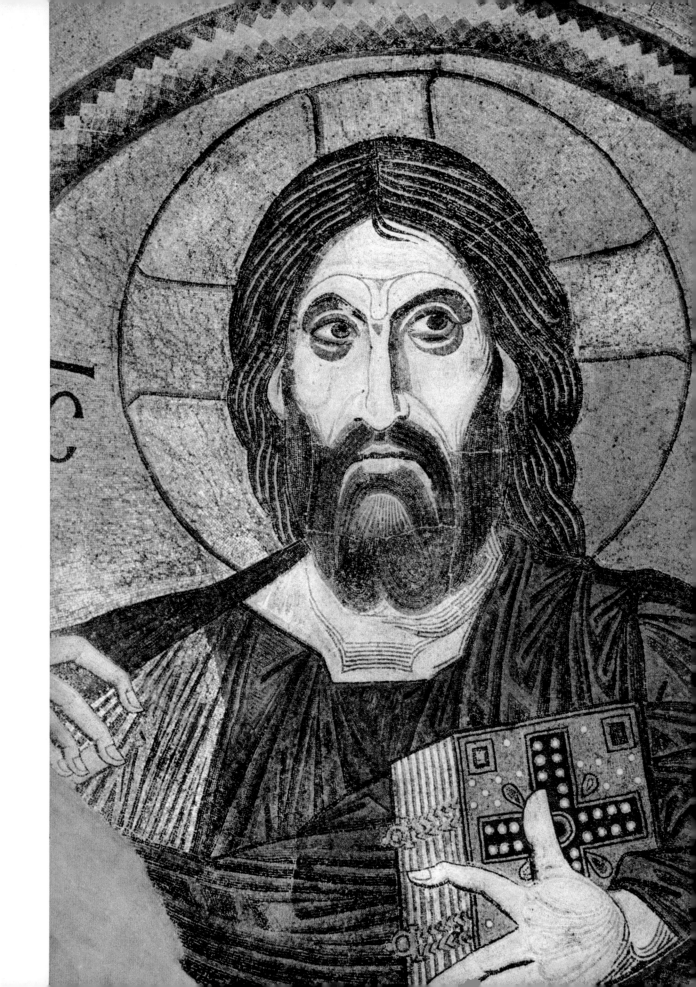

ist of Daphni is the
of the second Age of
aics (end of eleventh
he iconographic dispo-
fter the Quarrel of the
teen prophets unfurling
his awesome majesty,
er the dome like the
The hieratic aspect of
has something impla-
Western visitor does
. The minor grace of
t at Kaisariani speaks
him, perhaps not even

of self-preservation and partly because he has had to struggle, foot by foot, to defend his land, his family, and his religion. In this respect, too, his spirit is Greek.

Modern Greece is a bad bookkeeper of her ancient past, however fascinating her antiquity is to us. It is as though she did not want to be thrust backwards into her past under the guise of hypocritical pretexts. Aspiring to a European rôle, and forming a connecting-link between the West and the Middle East, she refuses to allow herself to be locked up under glass in a museum-case. She is, of course, today putting her tourist facilities in good order and building large hotels (the Amphitryon and the Bourzi in Nauplia; a palatial hotel at Sounion; the Centaur in Tsanga-rada; the Leto in Mykonos; the Spap in Olympia; and the Hotel of the Roses in Rhodes)—hotels whose bay-windows look out upon the splendor of Greek scenery.

It has taken a long time—longer than for other Mediterranean countries—for Greece to accustom herself to her own beauty. At Heracleum there is only one restaurant with a view of the gulf and the island of Dia. At Ioannina, pearl of the Epirus, on the shores of a lake steeped in Greek and Turkish legends, the traveler is led to a bedroom facing the courtyard. The visitor is similarly deprived of a view in Larissa, Athens, Patras, Corinth, Sparta, and Salonika. In the long run this would seem to be an error of judgment.

The highly unesthetic aspect of Greek cities which we discussed earlier is all the more difficult to explain since not only the Greece of Pericles but also the Greece of the knights—Medieval Greece—possessed in the highest degree the sense of majesty and feeling for the "indwelling spirit of place." To convince oneself of this, one has only

This horse whinnying at the morning light and awakening the anonymous groom sleeping under the shelter of his marble roof are, alas, only humble copies of the originals statues exiled to London. But their presence allows us to imagine the astonishing bustle of the divinities embarked on the upper deck of this big Greek ship rigged out to cross the centuries.

In Greece truth is often stranger than fiction. In other cases it rectifies it, enriching it with unexpected profiles.

Until the last few years it was not easy to become acquainted with the true face of Patmos. Illuminators and primitive painters had depicted the island where Saint John wrote the Apocalypse as a sort of round, flat shield placed on the sea. The prophet himself described it in hallucinating terms, with fire and brimstone under a blood-colored moon. The truth is pleasanter. Patmos offers boats the deepest gulf of the Dodecanese, as blue as the hills enclosing it are rose.

Saint John meditated in Saint Anne's grotto which is found on the large shoelace road leading from the port to the city above. With the rustic photo on the right we step from religious painting to military imagery. The mule of this peasantwoman of the small village of Andirrion walks on the horseshoe traces of more glorious steeds, those belonging to the French cavalry who stormed the Morea castle held by the Turks in 1828.

With the third photo reality lends a helping hand to the imagination: Victor Bérard, the inspired translator of The Odyssey, uses his poetic license to confuse the country of the Pheacians with the west coast of Corfu. He has Ulysses received by King Alkinous in the marvelous gardens which Bérard situates at the foot of the Laconese cliff. It must be admitted that the setting is worthy of Homer's heroes.

to wander about Mistra, the dead city of the four-teenth and fifteenth centuries, perched on the slopes of Taietos, and dominated by an imposing fortress. Mistra, of honey-blond walls accented sporadically with tufts of mauve, eerily evokes a Byzantine empire having collapsed from the savage onslaughts of the Orient. From its walls can be seen the valley of Eurotas, rich and peaceful, with orchards exhaling rosy mist in the mornings.

Sparta is there at the foot of Mistra, or rather, she was there at one time. Nothing remains today but a moral and a myth of supermen.

It is to Mistra that history is profoundly attached. The weight of five hundred years has undone its walls and houses, covered the narrow streets and stairs with weeds, collapsed its Byzantine cupolas, worn away the frescoes of its churches, and brought to ruins a palace whose high windows stare terrifyingly like empty eye-sockets. But a spiritual life has been kept alive in these silent monasteries where nuns, dressed in black in the style of the Touaregs, wander in white courtyards around which their narrow cells are grouped. Mistra goes on; Mistra lives.

Mistra will endure longer, no doubt, than Malvasia (also known as Monemvasia)—that Gibraltar of the Peloponnesian coasts, thrown up on the edge of the sea by a fantastic volcanic erup-tion. Malvasia is situated at the end of a harrowing road and on the route of a single boat-service which comes once a week from Piraeus. Her isolation has preserved one of the most beautiful spots on earth, but this very solitude gnaws away at the core of her being. A village, a veritable perfection in itself, is crumbling away under the walls of the fortress. The fortress and its Byzan-tine church overlook a mountainous, bare, hostile and deserted coast, which faces toward an East

The Propylaea or monumental entrances, built by Mnesicles after the completion of the Parthenon, already amazed Pericles' contemporaries who admired them as much as the temple and sometimes even more. After so many ravages of time and the elements during the centuries, the remains of the masterpiece still continue to make hearts beat faster. The young man Maurras was transported by its beauty like many others after him. I will let the image speak for itself. The photographer was able to seize upon the miraculous instant at sunset when the marble shafts become illuminated like so many altar candles. And remembering that these candles blaze the road leading to the temple of an antique virgin, it should be litanies of the Christian virgin which come to our lips:

House of gold...
Doorway to heaven...

formerly heavy with menace. The breath of life which still animates Mistra is lacking in Malvasia. The sweet wine of the islands no longer matures in her cellars. This stronghold, conquered by the great Villehardouin, is hopelessly doomed to a second death. But Malvasia—ruined, bloody in the setting sun or sea-green beneath an extravagantly romantic moonlight—bears witness of another Greece, masterly and robust, the one which so pleased Barrès.

One can never finish with enumerating the fortresses of the Frankish knights who held medieval Greece in a tight vise. Everything in such an enumeration alludes to the same prestige: Acrocorinth, Glarentza, the Kastro of Argos, the Palamedea fortress of Nauplia, the neo-Kastro of Pylos.

I shall never forget the walls of Rhodes, the palace of the Grand Masters and the ancient hospital, now a museum intelligently restored by the Italians. What happened during this epoch of history is beyond belief. A handful of men from the West came, conquered, kept, esteemed, and protected a land from the Oriental influence. This was a land where everything contrived to bring about their doom; where these men—too narrow-minded, overburdened with weapons, cut off from continental Europe—possessed, as advanced sentinels of Christianity, nothing with which to resist the Orient but an invincible faith and mad courage. The conquest and construction of these strongholds fall within the realm of the prodigious. They occupy only a relatively small place in the history of Greece, but they are significant: on this earth the great epochs of history have always been the work of an élite, feeble in number, but rich in audacity and intelligence.

Mycenae is still another example—three thou-

The monastery of the Pantanassa whose belfry has something of a lighthouse and watchtower about it, is part of the Byzantine city of Mistra founded in the fourteenth century by the despots Palaeologus or Cantacuzenes of the family of Byzantine emperors. The castle of these rulers dominates the city. Both edifices are built on the natural, jutting counterfort of Mount Taygetus which Guillaume de Villehardouin and his Frankish barons had already chosen in the thirteenth century for the site of their "golden burg," considered impregnable.

The plain of Sparta sprawls at the foot of Mistra, so renamed by the French who found Mezythra (cheese) too Greek and too pastoral, and changed it into Mistra, a French provincial dialect word with a prouder significance: "mistress."

From the Pantanassa church, built around 1430, which shelters today half a dozen nuns, the eye may contemplate with surprise the peaceful valley of the Eurotas where nothing remains of Spartan militarism. Among the church's frescoes of a late style is a resurrection of Lazarus painted in the colors of the Spartan countryside in the Spring: flaming red of the anemone, yellow of the laburnum, celestial blue of the periwinkle, rose of the flowering laurel, silvery green of the olive trees.

The Ceramic Cemetery owes its name to the principal industry of the suburb in which it is located. The wide tomblined walk along which are found the concessions of rich families of the fourth century has the melancholy charm of the Alyscamps promenade at Arles, but the sculptures still standing, or even their copies, make it an open-air museum.

In the theater of Dionysos the sculptures of Sileni decorating the procenium give evidence of the quality of sculpture in Nero's day. In these statues the decorative takes precedence over the sacred. The resemblance between the kneeling Silenus and Socrates is intentional.

Alcibiades described his master at Plato's banquet in these terms: "I shall say first that he closely resembles those Sileni to be seen in sculptors' studios."

sand years earlier than Mistra and Malvasia. Mycenae appears, in its construction and position, to be a sort of precocious, fortified castle. One awaits it with awe at the bend of a road, surging out of its legend, but it does not appear. The eye examines a deep valley in vain, but sees only two bare gray mountains and a pyramid of yellow stone.

This is obviously a fortress practicing the first rule of military art: "See without being seen." Mycenae does not reveal itself until the moment one arrives at the foot of its Cyclopean walls, facing the Gate of the Lions. A formidable defense system was organized at that time around the mountain top which was surmounted by several temples. A world unheard of rose out of the past. The city of the Atridae, suddenly laid bare where it had been buried with its pageantry of crimes and horrors, displays itself with great reluctance. It is a place for a searching meditation about the legends and destinies of dynasties which asserted their authority through crime.

Here it is that we take leave of beauty and things precious and elegant. Mycenae was a war machine conceived for war by warriors. From the palace terraces the imperial king surveyed the plain of Argos, the road from Corinth and the cove of Nauplia. Nothing escaped the eye peering from this eagle's nest. At one time an offensive force set forth from Mycenae and reached Asia Minor. How many Mycenaeans were there? If it is impossible to tell from the number of habitations, it is in any case certain that they were not numerous. But despite their limited numbers, their fame has spanned the centuries. They finally fell victim only to the Dorian hordes. When Mycenae sustained the Greek cause against Persia, she delegated an army of eighty men for the battle

The Kouros or Apollos of the archaic period are, perhaps, influenced by Egyptian art but their uniformity is only superficial. Jacques de Lacretelle very rightly spoke of a desire for individuality, a search for motion which make of these recruits standing at attention "troops in motion." Troops marching towards sovereign liberty, the almost literal flowering of Attic sculpture in the Golden Century. Aided by admirable materials and a technique of unrivaled virtuosity the Greek sculptor now has it in his power to stamp the fleeting instant with eternity: the quadriga caught in motion, the young woman carried off by her lover clutching her windblown skirt, are for me the realization of Faust's wish when he cried out after Helen, abducted by the Centaur: "Stand still, Instant. You are so beautiful!"

A comparison of these snapshots taken in museums, streets or fields gives proof of the perenniality of a certain Greek type, and especially of the faithfulness of the greatest artists to everyday reality. "Resemblance," far from shackling inspiration, gives wings to it.

of Plataea. At Thermopylae Leonidas had only three hundred men to withstand the army of Xerxes; at Marathon Miltiades challenged the army of Darius, which outnumbered his own ten to one; at Salamis the four hundred triremes of Themistocles sank the twelve hundred ships of the Persians.

Thus the real honor of Greece was inscribed in history: a victory of quality, of intelligence, of courage and of the beautiful and noble—that is to say, the contrary to what characterizes the world today: coarseness, bestiality, cowardice, hideousness and the mob.

This victory was, moreover, able to endure for centuries, to hold back the barbarians, to contain them or even to domesticate them. The disaster came only from Rome, at the hands of an emulator. From that day on, history took a fatal turn in which the fall of Byzantium (400,000 Turks and 500 ships against 8,000 Byzantines with 15 ships) constitutes only one episode.

The challenge taken up by the Frankish knights did not endure so long. If we are to accept the word of Kazantzakis, the country they conquered did not oppose these upright Christians. On the contrary, the country was too kind to them. Much too kind. The Greek wine lulled them into somnolence. Greek women pleased them. The became listless from the charm of this winsome and loving people. They succumbed, consciously or subconsciously, to the enchanting influence of the Greek countryside:—its odor of orange blossoms, the sweetness of its orchards and the shadow of its forests. On a soil which had drunk more blood than any other, which had heard so much clashing of arms, they heard only the flute of the shepherd and harvested only the flowers of spring. Softness overtook them, and the Turks routed

Because of a speech made by Demosthenes almost a century after the completion of the temple, the name of Parthenon (chamber of virgins), originally designating only one room in the edifice, was applied to the whole construction. The sculptor Phidias, the architect Ictinos and the contractor Callicrates built this masterpiece commissioned by Pericles, between 447 and 432. Was it ever consecrated to another cult than its own beauty? No one knows. What we do know, thanks to thorough technical analyses and to what is obvious anyway at first glance is that an exquisite curve tempers the severity of all its vertical lines, of all its horizontal arrises from its base to its vertex. Thus modeled, mellowed and caressed, the Parthenon is a body. It lives, it breathes, it captivates the mind, heart and senses like a Being, undoubtedly the most beautiful to have been offered for man's contemplation on earth.

them. In spite of all, it is this end devoid of grandeur which grips the heart—in Rhodes in particular.

There exists an absurd prejudice to the effect that Rhodes is not Greece, but part and parcel of Asia Minor, of Arabian Asia. Of course Rhodes has been influenced by the Turks. One has only to look at the minarets and that district of the old city where crowd together cobblers and the thousands of small artisans whose shops remind one irresistibly of Smyrna or Cairo. A highly varied population lives here, infused with foreign strains as the result of successive occupations. The most recent occupation, that of the Italians which ended only in 1947, produced a development of the natural and architectural beauties. This improvement gives Rhodes today a twenty-year advance over tourism in Crete and continental Greece. Arriving by boat in Rhodes, one is gripped by the force of its charm and strength. Encircled by its heavy, beige-colored wall, Rhodes slopes gradually down to the sea, terminating in a verdant headland. Lamartine asserts that he did not know a more smiling and fertile land. Naïve eyes search in vain for the silhouette of the famed Colossus at the port's entry. A doe and stag now stand on the spot where the Wonder of the World rested his feet until he was destroyed by an earthquake. His shadow, however, still looms over the city, mingled with those of the knights of the Order of St. John of Jerusalem. To medieval art, customarily heavy and aggressive, the climate and the muffled beauty of Rhodes have lent another dimension and noble finesse appropriate to these knights. To wander in their street, to enter the ancient hospital now converted into a museum, or to follow the maze of salons and corridors in the Magister's palace—any one of these is to

Hydra's welcome is delicious. In the perfect conch of its small oval port, the broad façades of its gleaming white houses unfurl from quay to peak of its golden mountain like so many welcoming flags. They were built for a handful of powerful families of corsairs at the end of the eighteenth century to amass their riches and to flout the Turks. At the first cry of revolt in 1821 the Condouriotis, the Miaoulis, and the Tombazis clans immediately headed up the party for freedom. Their one hundred and fifty swift galleys converted to warships became the terror of the enemy. But such a noble sacrifice and the rivalry of steamships emptied this fine horn of plenty. The corsairs' descendents have become sponge fishermen. Hydra is beginning to live off its charm. And very well at that. Painters from every country, scenarists, millionaires give it promise of a Saint-Tropezian future.

Crete has no "grand sculpture" in the true meaning of the word. But the minor arts — statuettes of women in glass and gold, figurines of bronze, engraved disks, and ceramic objects reveal a vituosity of hand, an eye for the real and a graphic imagination of a most captivating character.

The godesses are dressed in the style of the court with tightly laced corselets, bare bosoms, long flounced skirts. Their aprons draped on the hips and falling on the skirt in a shield-like oval are thought to be an adaption of the slip worn by the men of Libya.

The Phaestos terracotta disk is engraved with hieroglyphics certain of which, like the round shield and the feathered head, are not Minoan.

As for the picture of a group of bulls in the showcase of an archeological museum, it could be mistaken for a photograph of a herd of bulls crossing the Camargue delta.

discover oneself in the midst of a real medieval legend. It is as if, at any instant, one of those giants were going to spring from one of those inns whose façades are heavy with escutcheons and moldings of exquisite taste. These knights, bearing red coats-of-arms with two white crosses, battled heroically under the orders of Villiers de l'Isle-Adam against Suleiman II and died on Christmas Day 1522.

Christianity went no farther—at least not militarily. Rhodes marked its point of decline, but this point of decline is also sign the of a prestigious glory.

Everything in Rhodes is to be seen and experienced with pleasure: from Lindos and Empona, of which we have already spoken, to monasteries nestling in the woods. Orchards descend down to lovely, bare and deserted beaches where they quench their thirst at the edge of the sea; butterflies grace a valley filled with myriads of wild flowers. Like Crete, Rhodes could have lived independently, but her ancient heart beat for Greece. Today, having rejoined the mother country, she is a flower from the bouquet of Greece, sailing on the blue Aegean Sea facing Asia Minor. Asia Minor too has had its desires and hopes for Rhodes, but these are, without doubt, now lost forever.

Like Rhodes, Cos seems to be an error among the Greek islands of the Aegean. She is green and furrowed with luxuriant valleys and is near enough to Turkey to be able to make out the latter's wild, steep coast where white minarets point skyward. Cos is a favorite of doctors who come here to discover the souvenir of Hippocrates. A plane-tree more than fifteen yards in circumference is supposed to be the spot where the doctor-philosopher gave his consultations and lessons. Poor plane-tree! A broken column supports its

The Romans are not solely responsible for the "gigantism" of the Olympeion. As early as 515 B.C. Pisistrates had undertaken the construction of a colossal sanctuary dedicated to Zeus Olympian. Aristotle praised the ambition of this project interrupted by the fall of the tyrants. Four hundred years later, at the prompting of the King of Syria, Antiochus IV, the Roman architect Cossutius further enlarged the plans, chose the Corinthian order and Pentelican marble. The work, suspended at the death of Antiochus in 164 B.C., was resumed under Hadrian who consecrated the temple of Zeus in 131 A.D. for the inauguration of the Panhellenic festivities. These festivities have been perpetuated in our time at the beginning of Lent and after Easter in the shadow of sixteen columns still standing like a clump of tall palms fanning out in the pure blue of the sky.

If the Cretan dancers in their severe and pure costumes in the tones of red and black pottery carry on the classic style, the dancing girls of Megara recall the Greece of Byron, Chateaubriand, and the Orientalist painters. Their heads are covered with transparent scarves edged with lace and fringed with raw silk intermingled with gold threads. Their corselets are loaded with multicolored beads and their skirts are brightened by aprons embroidered in yellow, green and rose.

But classic or romantic, Greek peasant girls dance the same round to a rhythm similar to the Catalan sardanes which imitate the movement of waves on a sandy beach. The men dance separately and they are permitted a certain lyricism. The evzones of Athens remind us of Delacroix, of course, but doesn't this youth from Megara (the origin of the comedy) evoke rather a Toulouse-Lautrec subject, a sort of combination of Valentin and La Goulue doing the Greek cancan?

hardiest branch, hollowed out by billions of ants which have chewed away at this tree for more than twenty centuries. One feels that the tree does not want to die; that it is still resisting death out of sheer vanity. This affectionate spreading monster is hungry for glory—a glory it already has and, moreover, has retained through the ages.

But the plane-tree had better be careful! In the Pilion in the little gray town-square of Tsangarada another plane-tree is about to rob it of its record. All about the town, one of the prettiest forests of chestnut and oak that can be imagined is mutely giving encouragement to this rival tree.

Even without its famous landmark, Cos would continue to justify existence. The port is simple and charming, and the city breathes, within its rosy belt of large laurels, an air of respectable ease. The island is plump, a little soft like an Asiatic beauty. She does not gain more than a meager profit from the Greco-Roman ruins which reassure her of her past. The most beautiful of the mosaics discovered beneath the sand and earth which had invaded the temples of Asclepius have been shipped to Rhodes where they decorate the floors of the palace of the Grand Master. Cos allowed herself to be stripped without protest. It seems as though she sets more store on attracting the stranger by the sweetness of her climate, and by the renown of the springwaters and baths, which in ancient times made Cos a sort of Vichy.

In the archipelago of the Dodecanese, Cos is coupled with Rhodes whereas the ten other islands lead a separate existence. Among them, I consider it advisable, without prejudicing the others, to single out Calymna and Patmos.

Calymna is so Greek that she fills the heart with great satisfaction. From the boat that is anchored in front of the town, one can see only

A *bird's eye view from Delphi on the sacred delta of Krissa or Kirrha, lower valley of the Pleistos river where olive trees bigger than oaks spread out like a choppy sea. In the fifth century B.C. a site had been cleared in this profuse forest for the Hippodrome. The young Auriga with his eyes of enamel, today sheltered in the museum at Delphi, drove his chariot here. In the far distance the Bay of Itea plunges its blue steel blade into the flank of the wild Locris mountains. In the Middle Ages the port of Itea supplanted the antique port of Kirrha where boats used to anchor carrying marble for Delphian sanctuaries.*
Halfway up the slope is the small town of Amphissa where on market days one may watch the slow descent towards the sea of a solemn caravan of camels, unmindful of modern mechanics.

a big—a monstrous—rock; a port where small boats are grouped together; and a small town entirely painted in Prussian blue, in the form of an arc around the anchorage-basin. Here there is not one tree, nor one tuft of shrub. It is both inhuman and very beautiful. Calymna reveals her secrets only in the interior: two valley oases covered with orange-trees and fruit-trees; modest beaches encircled with oleander, and, separated from the island, a rock the size of Gibraltar and of Malvasia—looking out over Calymna and commanding a narrows.

Patmos, on the contrary, seems to be green. This is only an illusion. She is as hard as the other islands but her bay is admirable, deep and satisfying, and set off with a white village. From far away, the white and rose-gray silhouette of the monastery of St. John stands out on the summit of the island. The monastery occupies a high place in the Greek Church not only because of its erudition and piety but also because of the quality of the frescoes with which the church abounds. Shall I say that one can hardly conceive how in this calm, under cover of a deep grotto—it is indeed rather distressing—St. John was inspired with the Apocalypse. As for the vision, the apostle had been brooding over it in his soul. It was, without doubt, of little importance where it would be revealed to him.

The perfect position of the fortified monastery of Patmos leads to reflections similar to those concerning the sense of the "indwelling spirit of place" among the ancient Greeks. Christian Greece also possessed this theatrical sense—the taste for constructing religious edifices in those places where they asserted themselves with grandeur. Patmos is only one such example with which one can compare the convents of Hydra, hugging

These lions stretching their limbs in the sun like slender bloodhounds were sculptured in the sixth century B.C. in Naxos marble. They are the most famous ornament on the Island of Delos, one of the most famous places in the world. Apollo and Artemis were born here in the shade of a palm tree.

Delos, a religious center as important as Delphi, owes its resurrection to the work of the French School at Athens. Protected by its isolated position, its evocative power of antique life is as great as that of Pompeii but in an almost unbearable purity of light and lines. The lions of Naxos sat erect on their pedestals facing a lake which was filled in 1925. Swans and geese, Apollo's sacred animals glided on it. A legend preserves the image of the child Apollo riding on the back of a swan, prefiguration of Lohengrin. Five lions out of nine have remained in place. Another, removed in the seventeenth century, adorns the entrace to the Arsenal at Venice where Goethe admired it and dedicated a few lines to it.

This view of the Meteors presents a doubly Oriental aspect. It calls to mind, first of all, the columns on the top of which the Stylites, ascetics from Syria or Egypt, perched liked ibis or storks. And then the Chinese drawings of Tibetan landscapes.

The Varlaam monastery is forbidden to women. It was built at the beginning of the sixteenth century on the site of the hermit who gave it its name and who settled on this rock in the fourteenth century to flee a world troubled by the quarrels between the emperors of Serbia and Byzantium. Among the convents of Mount Athos (all as misogynic as Varlaam) we have chosen Pandokratoros whose buildings overhang the Aegean Sea. It was founded in 1270 by one of Michel Palaeologus' generals. Its library contains precious illuminated manuscripts.

The style of the sculptures adorning the pediments of Zeus' temple at Olympia around 460 B.C. provides the transition between the Dorian heroism of the ornamental façades of Aegina (480) and the plenitude of Attic classicism which flowered a little later on the Parthenon. Was it due to a Peloponnesian school or foreign artists influenced by Ionia? There have been many controversies on this subject and there will be many more.

What is uncontroversial is the equilibrium of the composition. On the west façade the combat between Centaurs and Lapithae is refereed by Apollo. On the right and left of the pacifying god the tangle of adversaries, centaurs' rumps, the Lapithae's vigor, the rise and fall of the veils of Hippodamia's companions are a marvel of expressive intensity and submission to a general rhythm which assigns to each statue the precise place of an instrument in an orchestra.

tightly on to hard rock; the convent of Poros, hidden in a forest of lemon-tress and pine; the one in Spetsai; the one in Osios Loukas on the edge of the road from Athens to Delphi; and, of course, those of Mount Athos and the Meteor. Everything in them incites to meditation which is not at all confined to little cells but rather on a vast scale—in the image of the world furrowed with valleys of tears and encircled by an eternal sea. Byzantine art accommodates itself to these perilous sites. The narrow and low chapels are as confining as tombs but are ornamented like reliquaries and plated with gold or silver. The features of the ikons have been obliterated by the kisses of the faithful throughout the centuries. These chapels smell of acrid olive oil from the burning votive lamps. Repudiating the whole secular world, prayers here are spoken and chanted by the popes and monks with their resonant, chesty voices. The smoke, the incense and the humidity have spoiled many of the Byzantine frescoes which adorn the walls of the monasteries of the METEORA but what remains possesses an intimate and touching charm.

Those who are interested in this epoch of Greek painting should not miss the church of Kritsa, near Ayios Nikolaos in Crete. Here, a miracle has preserved the ambiguous smiles of the Virgins, the tears of Christ and the fright of the wicked plunged into hell. Other frescoes of more recent origin decorate the convent of Pantanassa in Mistra. They afford, also, an idea of the original sanctity to which the artist-monks returned, having separated themselves from the world of living beings engaged in perpetual strife.

However, for sheer force, mosaic is the most effective medium. In the foremost rank is certainly the Christ Pantocrator of Daphni, the gem of

The whims of a photographer and of a springtime sky confer on this view of the Parthenon the strange quality of a daydream. Marble is reflected in marble, thanks to a sudden shower. And for an instant the colonnade blurs its own reality to rejoin its ghost.

Byzantium. This beautiful enraged face and these thin, agile hands soared above the faithful to remind them, rightly: how precarious was their existence; how much the faith was menaced; how pure and hard their religion had to be to withstand the onslaught of the waves from the depths of Islam.

This fear in which Byzantine and medieval Greece lived is absent from classical Greece. Of course, she kept herself armed and kept an eye fixed toward the East where the barbarians periodically sprang up.

But she did not know to be on guard against the North; against Macedonia which was going to swallow her up; and, even worse, against Rome who would suck her blood and try to disfigure her. Ancient Greece offered her splendor to everybody. Wherever she sinned with too much pride, the gods recalled her to order.

What remains of Olympia, apart from the "indwelling spirit of place," the setting, and a few pieces of the pediment of a temple?

Olympia is the first great humanitarian dream. When its games were announced, combatants abandoned their weapons and headed in long cohorts toward peaceful Arcadia. Thousands of pilgrims crossed seas and mountains to come and congregate in a beaten-earth stadium where the champions of the different city-states measured themselves one against the other—the champions of these city-states whose assembly formed the greatest Greece.

In those times there was the "truce of sport" just as later there was a "truce of God." The victors returned to their townsmen as heroes, and then they took up the war again where they had left off. One can hardly imagine today what an arousing place Olympia must have been at the times of the games.

At the extremity of the rock of Lindos the eastern wing of a Hellenistic portico describes two right angles. This geometry lesson on the brink of the wild blue yonder recalls the music lesson which Orpheus gave the wild beasts.
The sanctuary of Athena Lindia on its dizzy pedestal must have appeared to Saint Paul (who embarked nearby in a little port encircled by deserted cliffs) as the incarnation of Vanity.
For us, the daring grace of these columns is more likely to bring to mind the words of Shakespeare's Cleopatra:
"I'll set a bourn how far to be beloved."

The stadium is now a large funnel where people dig to find trophies of the victors and votive offerings. The columns, nearly two and a half yards in diameter, of the temple of Zeus lie on the ground, having collapsed like a house of cards. Rain, wind, cold and heat have slowly broken up the shell-containing stone which came came from nearby quarries. The graceful columns of the Palaestra; the Theocoleon; the Exedra of Herodes Atticus; the remains of the Pelopium; and the steles devoid of statues—all these re-create nothing of what ancient Olympia was like. Olympia is a ruin and wishes to remain a ruin.

Trees have invaded the sanctuary; a column has slipped; and the Alpheios and Kladeos Rivers have changed their beds.

There are, however, few places in Greece where illusion is so strong. The spirits of Olympia are present in this paradise once lost but later rediscovered. Earthquakes and the destructive fury of men have not been able to take away from the valley of the Alpheios, from blessed Arcadia, her perfume, colors, sky and magic. A unique harmony—arousing the soul's deepest gratitude—has been established between time and the quality of the landscape. It is not by chance that, for generations of poets, Arcadia has been the symbol of an earth where man, gorged with beauty, is free to pursue his own happiness. Nothing spoils the beauty of this valley of ferns and pines; where groves of cypress spread sharp black spots the length of the Alpheios, whose muddy waters flow between two banks of silver. Invaded by the countryside, but not crushed as at Delphi, the sanctuary of Olympian Zeus finds its true dimensions only at the Museum clinging to a sloping hillside.

Let us leave the Hermes—too well known to be

A *sort of heat mist seems to be suspended over Samos which is scarcely two miles from Asia Minor. In the deep and seemingly dead bay of Vathy stagnates an Oriental perfume. Something sweetish and irritating at the same time. There is an easy explanation. On the quays and anchored boats are cargoes of tobacco, casks and kegs of sweet wine which make up Samos' wealth. Egypt makes "Egyptian cigarettes" but does not grow tobacco. And what country, however distant, doesn't drink Samos' wine for dessert to accompany sweets?*
The island was at its zenith during the reign of Polycrates, "the wisest and most debauched of men," who comissioned Eupalinos of Megara to built an underground aqueduct and who tried to break the spell of his constant good luck by throwing into the sea the ring which assured him celestial protection. The next day Polycrates helped himself to a freshly caught fish at lunch and found his ring inside. This did not prevent him from being crucified in 522. But Samos remains a happy island.

The knights of Rhodes grouped their principal monuments in the Collachium, a sort of city within the city and separated from the market
chium, the Palace of the Grand Masters could serve as an independent fortress. The Order held its councils here. The square court, the open s
ones give it the character of Occidental architecture. Under the court large silos and several levels of vaulted storerooms permitted the storing o
Another precaution explains the many arches spanning the narrow streets of this walled city. It has nothing to do with decorative fantasy but we

wntown by a fortified wall. On the most elevated place in the Colla-
powerful arcades, the predominance of horizontal lines over vertical
munitions in case of siege.
measure against an enemy more terrible than the Infidels: earthquakes.

a surprise—and Nike, the Winged wictory, in order to contemplate the sculpture of the pediment—mutilated but surviving with a force which gives a measure of the setting of ancient Olympia. In the heart of the Greeks, Olympia symbolized truce, but a truce which was exalted. The contestants no longer vied with each other on a city-to-city basis, but rather as man to man, before the gods. The glory of bodies outshone all other glories. Compared with so much power, the masterpiece of Praxiteles is seen already to lean a bit toward love of self, of complaisance. It culminated in the summit of Greek sculpture—the summit of a pyramid of archaic sculpture, then classic, from which it emanated. Its grace is eternal, where as one would believe it to be fragile. It is probable that in the ring of the stadium, it would have been greeted with whistles from spectators in the tiers.

Like the Charioteer of Delphi, the Artemis of Piraeus and the Apollo Piombino of the Louvre, the Hermes of Praxiteles marks a point beyond which Greek sculpture could foreshadow nothing further. It became necessary either to imitate it or to perish. Greece did both, aided in large part by artists from Italy who covered Greece with their copies. The break of continuity is too obvious to escape even the least practiced eye. Greek sculpture is also severe for the art of Rome whose imperfections it underlined by creating an intoxication other than that of the "indwelling spirit of place." For in the last analysis, Greek sculpture speaks to us of a people as if they were still living. The fabulous Greeks are there, and we see them from birth to death, reaching for a common goal: perfection. Children, warriors, goddesses, nymphs, gods and heroes are all animated by the same impetus.

The present vestiges of Apollo's temple at Delphi are of gray-blue limestone and date from the fourth century. Few histories are as eventful as this sanctuary's, coveted by all the large states which fought with equal fanaticism for the possession of the property of the Oracle who dictated the destinies of the Greek world. Natural catastrophes such as lightning and earthquakes added to the damage done by men's looting. Restorations followed on destructions and the temple momentarily recaptured its former splendor. Today archeologists try more or less successfully to restore what is restorable. This immense debris, wreckage of a multisecular disaster, is beginning to look like its old self again.

The monastic republic of Athos is governed by unalterable but widely varied laws. It thus offers to very different temperaments work suited to each one's religious vocation. There are two absolute imperatives: 1) The wearing of a beard and long hair, the latter to be knotted into a chignon and hidden under a cap or scouffa. 2) The obligation to pray eight hours out of every twenty-four.

The relatively short beard of the monk reading beside the road leading to the domed convent indicates his age: he must be a young novice called Dokimos after his black robe. On the other hand, the old man descending the steep mountain path could be a gyrovaque, a begging, vagabond monk.

A gyrovaque, too, the monk sitting in the bow of the boat heading for Thosos, one of the islands closest to Athos. The monks go there frequently for shopping and for a bit of modern day air.

During some of the important celebrations like Easter the splendor of the orthodox rite emerges into the busy streets of modern Athens, reviving the riches of Byzantium.

A mysterious smile graces the masterpieces of the archaic period whereas the classic period contrasts sharply with it by possessing a calm forever to be described as "Olympian." What is remarkable is that beneath this calm is hidden a scarcely discernible quivering. Passion is not far off, but being transient is necessarily left to the great myths which aroused people of that time. Greek sculpture, such as it is revealed by the archæological museum in Athens, the museum of the Acropolis, the museum of Olympia, as well as several charming provincial museums, is a bewitching sculpture wherein the supreme grace is surrounded by magic. One can only give way before Greek sculpture with the poignant sentiment that the Greeks of this period reached a summit, forever afterwards unattainable. Man has been able to invent a thousand other forms and torture art consciously or subconsciously; but there he lived his greatest dream.

Thus ancient Greece appears to the foreigner not as the end of the world, but rather as the end of a world. After her, the history of civilizations seems no more agitated than convulsive palpitations. A unique form of equilibrium between man and his thought manifested itself in several temples and pieces of sulpture which have spanned the centuries, forever recalling us to order. A way of life also remains, which is another "call to order" because joy and contemplation—in order to be practiced—required nothing else except a certain sky and a certain purity of heart.

It is possible that some day machines and space will give back to man the happiness he has lost. This is possible, and we should hope for it even amidst our disbelief. But what is probable is that Greece, through her structure, her traditions and her character, will remain— whether she

With his enamel, clear, deep set eyes, his moving mouth, the ephebe of Anticythera (the name of the place where he was discovered) is perhaps the admirable copy of a work of the fourth century B.C. Some archeologists believe it to be the effigy of Paris. Others that of Hermes. We would like to believe the latter and that this somnambulist diver, his eyes fixed on the Invisible, was really the god "leader of souls" guiding, like Heurtebise in Jean Cocteau's film Orpheus, the souls in his charge across the "zone" separating the world of the living from that of the dead.
Greek bronze workers used four sorts of patina: green, black, blue and the choicest of all — hepatizon, livercolored.

wishes to or not — the country where one will re-learn lost gestures; where peasant-girls will spin wool while guarding their flocks; where only little donkeys will be able to bring the traveler up from the port of Santorin to his village; where automobiles will be unknown on the islands; where coastal navigation in the Sporades and the Cyclades will continue to be carried on by loaded ships with red sails; where the taste of bread, of oil, of olives and sheep-cheese will be better in the country than in the city; where in village inns the radio will be turned off in the evenings in order to give place to two bouzouki players whose musical strains will make men dance; where the door of a house which opens to a stranger will set in motion sacred rites of hospitality. For the past as for the present, for all she offers with so much prodigality, Greece remains a part of our reason for living.

I *have already said it: "If the Parthenon exalts, the Theseus instructs." To fully appreciate it one must step back and look at it, as in this picture, from a certain distance in a subdued light which enhances its severe Doric style.*

*O*lympia's Altis, today a park, was originally a grove of wild olive trees marked out, according to the legend, by Herakles for his father. After the victory of Salamis, the Greeks decided to build on this site, where Zeus had only an altar, the largest and most beautiful of all temples dedicated until then to the master of the gods. The Elean architect Libon supervised the work from 468 to 457 B.C. When the sanctuary was finished, Phidias' famous statue sculptured in ivory and gold was placed there. It was the "Olympian Zeus," one of the seven wonders of the world. The temple remained standing until the sixth century in spite of Christian persecutions. It took an earthquake to destroy it. The shell stone used to build it has suffered so much from time and the elements that a restoration is not possible — and, it must be admitted, it is better this way. From this field of ruins arises a serene gravity which the painter Poussin recaptured, although he never visited Olympia, in his evocation of an imaginary Arcadia.

MAJOR DATES IN GREEK HISTORY

B. C.

2000-1500
The Hellenes, a branch of the Indo-European peoples, occupy the lands of the eastern Mediterranean inhabited by the Aegeans and the Cretans.

1500-1100
Achaean (or Mycenaean) civilization, centered in Mycenae, in Argolis.

1400
Burning of the palace of Knossos (Crete).

about 1180
Trojan War, basis of Homer's epic.

1100
Dorian invasion of the Peloponnesus, home of the Achaeans.

1074-1044
Dorian, Aeolian and Ionian colonies in the islands of the Aegean Sea and in Asia Minor.

1066
The Dorians attack Athens. Death of King Codrus.

820
Lycurgus at Sparta (aristocratic constitution).

776
First Olympic Games.

743-724
First war of the Messenians against the Spartans.

734
The Greeks colonize Italy and Sicily.

704
Birth of the poet Archilochus at Paros.

645
Messenians defeated in second war.

about 640
Birth of Thales, first Greek philosopher-scientist.

621
Legislation of Dracon in Athens.

600
Foundation of Marseilles by mariners from Phocaea in Asia Minor.

594
Legislation of Solon in Athens. Suppression of debt slavery.

580
Birth of mathematician Pythagoras in Samos.

561
Pisistratus, tyrant of Athens. Formulation of text of Homeric poems, dating back to the ninth century.

510
The Spartans occupy Athens and overthrow Hippias.

507
In Athens, the constitution of Clisthenes, foundation of democracy.

506
Athens repels an expedition of Spartans, Thebans, and Chalcidians.

499
Revolt of the Ionians against the Persians.

495
Birth of Sophocles, tragic poet. Victory of the Greeks under Miltiades at Marathon.

490
Darius leads a first expedition against the Greeks (600 ships, 110,000 men).

480
Second Median War (Xerxes). The Persians in Athens. Victory of the Greeks, commanded by Themistocles, at Salamis. Birth of Herodotus, historian and traveler.

479
League of Delos, headed by Athens (Confederation of Cities) against the Persians. Later this League became a veritable Athenian empire.

478
Athens reconstructed and equipped with a port.

476

Pindar writes the ode to Theron.

469

Birth of Socrates.

462

Abolition of the Areopagus, which had limited popular sovereignty.

461

Pericles comes to power. Athens has a population of 400,000.

about 460

Birth of Democritus, philosopher and mathematician.

454-438

Building of the Parthenon.

about 450

"Prometheus Bound," tragedy by Aeschylus. Myron's statue of "The Discus-Thrower".

450

Phidias, at the age of 42, directs work on the Acropolis.

449

Under the command of Cimon, the Athenians win victory over Persians. End of the Median wars.

446

Peace of Thirty Years between Athens and Sparta - Sophocles (died 405).

440

Youth of Hippocrates, father of medicine.

431-404

Peloponnesian War.

431

First invasion of Attica by the Spartans.

430

Death of Pericles. Plague in Athens.

427

Birth of Plato.

425

Last invasion of Attica by the Peloponnesians.

421

Peace of Nicias between Spartans and Athenians. Comedies of Aristophanes.

420

"Oedipus Rex" of Sophocles.

415-413

Sicilian expedition. Destruction of Athenian army.

413

Spartans occupy Deceleum, in Attica.

411

Oligarchical government of the Four Hundred, then of the Five Thousand.

410-407

Naval victory in the Hellespont and near Cyzicus, Alcibiades destroys the Spartan fleet.

406

Death of Euripides.

404

Lysander (Sparta) captures Athens. End of the Peloponnesian War. Government of the Thirty Tyrants. Death of Alcibiades.

403

Restoration of democracy. Thrasybulus.

400-394

Spartan victories in Asia Minor against the Persians.

399

Death of Socrates.

395-387

Athens, Corinth, Thebes and Argos unite against Sparta.

395

Spartans under Lysander are defeated at Haliartus, in Boeotia.

387-386

Peace of Antalcidas.

384

Birth of Aristotle at Stagira.

379

War of Thebes against Sparta.

375

Death of Hippocrates.

370

Invasion of the Peloponnesus by the Thebans. Messenia regains independence.

362

Epaminondas invades the Peloponnesus. His victory and death at Mantinea.

360

Philip II accedes to the throne of Macedonia.

357

Philip seizes the Aegean coast.

355-346

Third sacred war against the Phocians. Philip conquers Thessaly but fails at Thermopylae - Demosthenes.

348

Philip conquers Thrace.

347

Death of Plato.

346

Peace between Philip and the Athenians.

339-338

New sacred war. Defeat of the Athenians at Chaeronea. Philip is proclaimed general of the confederated Greeks.

338-326

Government of Lycurgus in Athens.

336

Assassination of Philip. Alexander, pupil of Aristotle, succeeds him.

335

Thebes destroyed by Alexander.

334

Alexander conquers Asia Minor with 30,000 infantrymen, 5,000 cavalrymen plus engineers.

333

Victory of Alexander at Issus. He takes possession of Phoenicia, Palestine, Egypt. Founding of Alexandria.

332

Fall of Tyre.

330

Assassination of King Darius. Uprising of the Spartans.

328-321

Voyage of Pytheas, Phocaean explorer, to the British Isles.

327-325

Expedition of Alexander to the frontiers of India.

323

Death of Alexander in Babylon. Perdiccas becomes regent. Antipater commands in Macedonia and in Greece. Ptolemy governs Egypt. Euclid.

323-322

War of Lamiacum. Capitulation of Athens. Death of Demosthenes. Death of Diogenes.

314

First conflicts over the division of Alexander's empire.

307

Athenian democracy restored by Demetrius Poliorcetes.

306

Epicurus in Athens.

301

Aeolian League.

about 300

Birth of the poet Theocritus.

300

Birth of the physician Herophilus, who later taught in Egypt.

287

Birth of Archimedes.

280-278

Invasion of the Gauls and their defeat.

272

Death of Pyrrhus in Argos.

262

The King of Macedonia captures Athens.

222

Macedonia holds sway over Greece.

212

Death of Archimedes.

211-205

First Macedonian war. Alliance of Macedonia (Philip V) and Hannibal.

209-194

Second Macedonian war.

205

Peace between Rome and Philip and his allies.

197

Defeat of Philip by Flamininus.

196

At Corinth, Flamininus proclaims Greek independence.

179

Perseus comes to power in Macedonia.

172-168

Third Macedonian war.

150

Heron, engineer, who later invented the principle of the steam-engine.

146

Victory of the Romans over the Achaean League. Capture of Corinth. Greece is subjugated by Rome.

131

Revolt of the slaves in Attica.

86

Capture of Athens by Sulla; pillaging of the city.

48

Rivalry between Julius Caesar and Pompey. Victory of Caesar at Pharsalus.

31

Reign of Augustus. Greece is the Roman province of Achaia.

A. D.

First Century

St. Paul preaches in Athens and Corinth - St. John at Patmos (Dodecanese).

54

Nero plunders Greek monuments and takes them to Rome.

117-138

Emperor Hadrian visits Greece and embellishes Athens.

about 170

Description of Greece by Pausanias.

249-251

The Goths menace the frontiers.

253

Beginning of fortifications around Athens, under Valerian.

260-268

Invasion by the Goths.

273

Destruction by fire of the library of Alexandria, containing many Greek manuscripts.

324

Constantine in Constantinople. Christianity becomes state religion.

393

Last Olympic Games.

395

Invasion of Greece by the Goths (Alaric). Destruction of Eleusis, occupation of Athens.

467-477

Invasion by the Vandals.

549

Invasion by the Slavs.

Sixth Century

Closing of the Schools of Philosophy. Transformation of temples into churches.

717

Leo III, Emperor of Byzantium.

727

Revolt of the Greeks.

780-800

Struggle against the Slavs.

842-867

Michael III defeats the Slavs.

976

Emperor Basil II defeats the Bulgars at Thermopylae. Emergence of the Albanians.

1054

Schism between the Greek and Latin churches.

1080

Norman invasion.

1204

The Crusades. Conquest of Greece by the Crusaders. Villehardouin on the west coast of the Peloponnesus.

1205

Guillaume de Champlitte, first prince of Morea.

1206

The Venetians occupy Methone and Chaeronea.

1218

Death of Villehardouin, who had succeeded Guillaume de Champlitte. His son, Geoffrey II, recognized as Duke of Achaea by Constantinople.

1267

Charles d'Anjou acquires from Baudouin II the rights to the principality of Morea.

1311

Capture of Athens by the Catalans.

1375

Sultan Mourad captures part of Macedonia.

1453

End of the Byzantine Empire.

1456

The Turks capture Attica. Struggles with Venice.

1503

Peace between Venice and the Sultan.

1522

Defeat, at Rhodes, of the Knights of St. John.

1685-1699

Conquest of Morea by the Venetians. The Doge Morosini lays siege to Athens and plunders the Acropolis.

1715

Achmed III recaptures Morea.

1770

Russo-Turkish War - revolt of the Greeks.

1774

The Albanians ravage Greece; they are finally defeated by Hassan Pasha.

1800

Study of the Parthenon by Lord Elgin, who shipped important pieces of sculpture to England.

1821

Uprising of the Greeks against the Turks. Massacre of the Greeks at Constantinople.

1822

National Assembly of Epidaurus - Massacre at Chios - Capture of Athens by the Greeks.

1824

Byron dies at Missolonghi.

1826

Recapture of Athens by the Turks under Rashid Pasha.

1827

New assemblies of Epidaurus and Troezen - Intervention by England, France and Russia - The allied fleet destroys the Turko-Egyptian fleet at Navarino.

1828

Evacuation of Morea by Ibrahim Pasha.

1830

Founding of a Greek state, governed by a prince.

1831

Assassination of Capo d'Istria, who, four years earlier, was President of the Greek Republic.

1833

Otho of Bavaria becomes Prince of Greece at the age of 18 and selects Athens as his capital.

1843

Revolution in Athens, followed by government of Kolettes.

1850

Blockade of Greece by England - mediation by France.

1854

Crimean War - agitation in Greece - occupation of Piraeus by Franco-English fleet.

1862

Uprising of Nauplia - overthrow of Bavarian monarchy.

1863

William of Denmark is proclaimed King of Greece under the name of George I.

1864

Ionian islands join the kingdom.

1866-1869

Uprising of Crete against the Turks.

1869

Paris conference and resumption of diplomatic relations with Turkey.

1881

Treaty of Constantinople. Thessaly and the Arta district ceded to Greece.

1893

Inauguration of Corinthian Canal.

1897

Greco-Turkish war and defeat of Greek army in Thessaly. Treaty of Constantinople. Autonomy of Crete.

1909

Revolt of Athenians. Military dictatorship.

1912

War against Turkey. Entry of Greeks into Salonika, advance into Epirus.

1913

Assassination of George I in Salonika. Accession to power of Constantine. November 15, Treaty of Athens (acquisition of Crete, of part of Epirus, of Macedonia and western Thrace).

1914

Neutrality of Greece.

1915

Rupture between Venizelos and the King. Allies in Salonika.

1917

Abdication of Constantine. Venizelos comes to power.

1920

Treaty of Sèvres : Greece will administer the territory of Smyrna, eastern Thrace and the islands. Fall of Venizelos. Return of Constantine.

1921-1922

Greco-Turkish War in Asia Minor.

1922

Entry of Turks into Smyrna. Abdication of Constantine. Accession of George II. Armistice of Macedonia.

1923

Abdication of George II.

1924

Venizelos leaves Greece.

1924

Proclamation of the Republic. Plebiscite. National Constituent Assembly.

1928

New ministry of Venizelos.

1933

Venizelos, defeated at the elections, leaves office.

1935

Restoration of George II.

1940

Greek ship torpedoed by the Italians. Invasion of Greece by army of Mussolini.

1941

Italian army repulsed. Intervention of Germany. Occupation of Greece by Hitler's troops.

1942

First Free Greek Brigade at El Alamein.

1943

Greeks participate in Tunisian campaign and in island of Samos.

1944

Greeks land at Taranto. Occupation of Rimini.

1944-1945

Liberation of the Dodecanese and islands of the Aegean Sea.

1944

Germans leave Athens. Regency of Archbishop Damaskinos.

1946

Return of George II.

1947

Death of George II - Accession of King Paul I.

1948

Return of the Dodecanese Islands to Greece.

PRINTED IN FRANCE THE 15th OF AUGUST 1961
THE HELIOGRAVURE WAS PRINTED BY BRAUN
OF MULHOUSE AND THE ILLUSTRATIONS
IN COLOR BY DRAEGER OF PARIS.